Restoring Spiritual Health

How To Avoid
The Bitterness
of
Christianity

By

M. D. Ewing

Restoring Spiritual Health

How To Avoid The Bitterness of Christianity

By

M. D. Ewing

Restoring Spiritual Health
How To Avoid The Bitterness of Christianity

Copyright© 2012 by Enlightenment Publishing, LLC

All rights reserved. No part of this publication may be reproduced, stored in a retrieval system, or transmitted in any form or by any means–electronic, mechanical, photocopying, recording, or otherwise–without the prior written permission of the copyright owners and Enlightenment Publishing, LLC, New Haven, Michigan 48048.

Scripture quotations taken from the Holy Bible, New Living Translation, copyright © 1996, 2004, 2007 by Tyndale House Foundation. Used by the permission of Tyndale House Publishers, Inc., Carol Stream, Illinois 60188. All rights reserved.

Scripture quotations taken from the Amplified® Bible, Copyright © 1954, 1958, 1962, 1964, 1965, 1987 by The Lockman Foundation Used by permission." (www.Lockman.org)

ISBN 978-0-9855490-2-2

Published By:

Enlightenment Publishing, LLC

P.O. Box 480442

New Haven, MI 48048

enlightpub@gmail.com

http://enlightpub.wix.com/enlightenment

Contents Within The Book

The Author's Thoughts — i

Thanks and Dedication — vii

Introduction — Page 13

Chapter 1
Hearing Him — Page 36

Chapter 2
A Blessing & A Tragedy — Page 59

Chapter 3
Beware of False Prophets — Page 163

Chapter 4
Avoid Controlling Spirits — Page 198

Chapter 5
The Essence of Salvation — Page 213

Chapter 6
Pure Faith — Page 232

Chapter 7
Religion vs. Realization — Page 245

Chapter 8
Final Analysis - Real Talk — Page 265

THE AUTHOR'S THOUGHTS

Anyone who has been in close company with me or my family knows I am passionate about many things. Passionate about family: how a husband must love, honor, and cherish his wife and children with great appreciation and esteem – not just by words only – but in demonstrating this lifelong obligation (with his wife and children providing that same compassion with admiration and respect).

Passionate about men being men indeed: not by the consent and sanctioning of others, but by discovering their true identity as a man and understanding their God-given purpose in this world; understanding the importance of education and hard work; accepting personal responsibility; striving to improve and develop good personal character; and being a good influence and encouragement toward all people (especially other men). These are the qualities I strive to live by, practice, and inspire in my own son.

Passionate about women (especially because I have three daughters of my own) respecting and loving themselves: respecting their own bodies; respecting and loving their own husband and children; not allowing the world around them to influence and define who they are and what they are supposed to be, but allowing God to define them, true fathers to protect and assemble them, their mothers to shape and mold them, and education and knowledge to fabricate and empower them.

But there is something else I am strongly passionate about – something that I am strongly committed to, especially after having many years of training and personal experience. Persevering through troubling times while enjoying the precious moments in life, I am passionate about teaching God's people and illuminating the reality and freedom in Christianity. All too often, we converse about Christ, we have the appearance of

Christianity, we know how to sing and dance for Christ and raise our hands in a solemn ceremonial fashion; but there is a famine of craving for biblical knowledge as a personal obligation as it relates to Christian living and proper conduct.

We create a mental note that living a life pleasing to God according to His Word is old-fashioned, obsolete, and archaic (as if God is requiring us to impersonate the physical aspects of old biblical times); or we make a note in our mental diary that Christian behavior is only for those who preach and teach the gospel of Christ or for those who are really deep into God. But the scriptures plainly enlighten everyone who has unified with Christ that we have become His new creation (reprogrammed as new human beings who get a brand-new start in life); the old way of living is vanishing away to make room for the new you. (1 Corinthians 5:17) However, we have restrictions on how much of Christ's teachings we allow to mold us (as clay in the hands of a potter); rather, we attempt to re-create the old nature of living in union with our new spiritual temperament using the imperfection of mankind as an excuse to live uncivil as our desire to grow spiritually in God becomes impoverished.

Because of our human way of thinking and our charismatic personality, the challenge to mature in Christian faith goes unformatted, especially when we can offer our talents, gifts, and money in exchange for our body, soul, and spirit which 1Thessalonians 5:23 tells us to safeguard and keep untarnished, until our Lord Jesus Christ comes again. For this cause, we select our own standards of living and substitute it as Christ's standards for living. No, I don't preach perfection because I can't live perfection, but I do teach maturity because we all can mature as Christians.

Maturity comes through a lifetime of experiences and in making many mistakes; but, instead of making excuses, we learn from our blunders, making it our business to ask God for repentance and His strength to endure and persevere. Christ sustains us, His word teaches us, but the test of life shapes us. I strongly believe that if you have not been tested as a Christian then you cannot be trusted to lead in Christian ministry. Before Christ ever preached one message or taught one lesson about God, He was tempted/tested in the wilderness for 40 days and 40 nights. Alone there in the wilderness, he had to rely on God and God only – and he endured. No pastors or prophets, no bishops or elders, no evangelists or teachers. He was there – ALONE – with God. The basic principles of Christianity are accepting Christ and His teachings about God, striving to live according to God's standards, enduring hardships, and developing a personal relationship with God according to his word (a personal relationship between you and God).

Yes, we have various leaders, brothers, and sisters who are willing to stand with us, that is until someone becomes offended (emotionally injured) with sometimes trivial issues, then their willingness to relieve and support your cause is lost in a pool of human insensitivity. And there you are, all alone, unaided in the physical but never unaccompanied in the spiritual. No offence to anyone, but the naked truth has been clothed. The carnal nature of man, in its most elaborate condition, is full of hate and envy; therefore, we must learn to personally rely on the Spirit of the living God at all times.

This challenge to become acquainted with God is by no means an excuse to replace the need for Christian association and unity in the body of Christ; but it is a sure way to recognize the difference between the prominence of God and the error and foolishness of civilization, including many who profess the name of Jesus in the body of Christ. Seeking a personal relationship with God takes serious effort and is vital to the stability of our well-being and the longevity of our faith; and although many neglect this important phase of their Christianity, it is the surest way to maintain your relationship with Christ, unwavering and unbroken, when everything and everyone else around us seems to be falling apart.

THANKS & DEDICATION

First and foremost, I thank God and His Son, Jesus Christ, for life and good health, for salvation and liberation. I also thank Him for the ability to write and express to you in love the hidden and unacknowledged realities of Christianity within the structure of the facilities we called "The Church." What I express through the pages of this book is more relative to actual accounts than a sum of unfounded opinions, and the genuineness of what is expressed has been lived (as a testimony) through the lives of countless souls. I'd like to acknowledge and thank my wife, Bridget, and children (Zaria, Zanetta, Zashanae, and Mitch Jr.) for their participation, patience, and prayers in this, my attempt to encourage and educate many on a much-needed subject. This book describes the elements of Christianity to include the various pitfalls that arise for a person of faith, and the importance of establishing a solid foundation in Christ – not just seeking to be inaugurated as a member of an organization for attendance and financial obligation purposes, but to create a personal relationship within Christ to prolong the existence, durability, and growth of our faith.

I dedicate this book to you; but more importantly, I thank God for giving you the wisdom and understanding to digest this literature, in hopes that both you and I will thoroughly and continually examine the nature of our faith through the eyes of the already founded Word of God. I pray that this book presents itself as a sanitizing and disinfecting agent that will aid us in cleansing our minds/bodies and serve as a catalyst to oppose the many misfortunes and calamities gained through the flawed practices of Christianity. May you be rejuvenated and replenished in your quest and desire to continue serving the true and living God.

INTRODUCTION

The fundamental nature of this book is to educate new believers, as well as mature Christians, about their personal responsibility to grow in faith and in the grace of God. The offices of the apostle, prophet, evangelist, pastor, and teacher, as described in Ephesians 4, are positions of leadership that God has designated to lend a hand or be of assistance in maturing and establishing his people. It is not biblically mandatory that every ministry should have every office implemented in their church simultaneously, as long as one or more of those entities are fully serviceable in ministry.

However, anyone who serves in these positions must be people who are spiritually developed (not babes) in Christian faith. Possessing spiritual gifts is not a sign of maturity. Having the ability to influence people by prophesying, teaching, preaching, or working diverse miracles does not indicate a great leader. Even in biblical history, during the days of Moses, Pharaoh had sorcerers and magicians in Egypt, such as Jannes and Jambres, who emulated the miracles of God by turning water into blood, as did Moses who was accompanied by his brother Aaron. Though these sorcerers possessed spiritual gifts, their gifts did not establish them as leaders in Egypt, nor did these gifts make them substantially great. They were just servants. Nonetheless, God did not craft His leaders to become miniature gods in Christ's stead.

In other words, as God's leaders we should never be the center of attention in ministry, neither should we be the main focus of your faith. Our interest should always be toward God's people in supporting, serving, and loving them, and not for them to become devoted servants to our private agendas in support of those who desire to build personal kingdoms here on earth. How are we as leaders supposed to love God's people? 1 John 3:18 instructs all of us not to love simply in theory or insincere dialogue but to show irresistible care in practice, sincerity, and genuineness. Leaders' heartfelt love for people should never be measured by how much a person can or cannot accomplish for them.

Many Christians today grant too much authority to religious figures, such as pastors or prophets, with the mindset that these people of interest have some special connection with God that no one else in this life can possess. Because of this way of thinking, many cast their hopes, faith, and devotion at the feet of their leaders in expectation of receiving God's favor and blessings, believing that if they can demonstrate total reliance and commitment to a man, woman, or organization, one day God will rain blessings from Heaven upon their life and be well pleased with them.

No one should ever be so mesmerized or influenced by their pastor or leader to the point that nothing else matters except what that pastor or leader utters or implements. Remember, 1 Peter 1:21 informs us that through Christ we believe in God, who resurrected Christ from the dead and bestowed upon Him honor and reverence so that our individual faith and hope might be secured and centered in God and no one else. Though it is very important to show value, love, and honor toward those who truly labor in Christ, all too often Christians translate the word "honor" to mean "worship, praise, and highly exalt."

One of the key signs that illustrates whether or not a person's faith, hope, and trust is solely dependent upon their pastor or leader is evident in what usually proceeds from their lips, most often heard as: "My pastor this..., or my pastor that..., or my pastor said..., or my pastor believes..., or my pastor does it this way...," and the emphasis of "what Christ taught" or "what Christ said" is absent. This disease is what I call "pastoritis" or "manism," which describes those who build their faith based on the words of a man or woman without researching Christ's spoken word and representing the one who died for their sins. Even to the point that if they were shown or given biblical references by another person, other than their pastor, those with "pastoritis" will automatically reject and refuse anything outside the consent of their leader. This is because many have been misled to believe their pastors/leaders are the only ones who are equipped and capable to teach them. However, the Bible does illustrate an abundance of people competent enough to preach and teach God's Word, not limited to only one or two people in one or two places.

One quick thought: Where was God before the birth of your pastor or leader? Or did God only appear when your pastor or leader came into existence? Those statements were made to amplify this one point: God's Word is the teacher, the author, and finisher of our faith – the reason for our existence and the continuance of our survival. In my 25 years of salvation and ministry, this disease is by far the most common error observed among young and older Christians, and one of the deadliest traps to stunt spiritual growth, which often leads to "the bitterness of Christianity."

In today's society, this is the approach that is taught to Christians, usually by creating and adopting biblical concepts, such as the relationship between Elijah and Elisha, which began in the book of 1 Kings 19. The prophet Elijah was instructed by God to anoint Elisha to take his place as the prophet in the region. Elijah didn't choose Elisha to become his spiritual pupil, nor did Elijah ask Elisha to serve him in order to gain the favor and blessings of God. Elisha's servitude toward Elijah was strictly optional, and there is no biblical reference anywhere that states it was mandatory for Elisha to serve Elijah just to develop a close bond with God; however, Elisha accepted his vocation from God, choosing to follow Elijah. His maturity and development as a prophet required him to learn from a more experienced prophet, which united Elijah and Elisha as close acquaintances.

As time elapsed, Elisha became the prophet God designed him to be. What Elisha received from Elijah was not the spirit of a man (as inaccurately articulated), but the spirit and power of God through a wealth of (human) experience in the life of Elijah. It was much more visible in the life of Elisha and demonstrated by a greater number of miracles performed by Elisha (greater works for a greater purpose). This story, including the relationship between Moses and Joshua, as well as other stories, were not intended to be substituted and used as the official guidelines for serving our leaders.

In every example of these types of biblical relationships, one person was being replaced by another, and these leaders never selected their successors, nor required their protégés to support them financially or serve them for personal pleasures. Jesus stated in the book of Mark 10:42 that the rulers of this world would exercise control and dominance over their people; becoming lords over them and holding them in subjection to self-governing rules; but admonished his disciples not to abuse their authority over those under them.

Jesus concluded His thoughts by sharing with His disciples that they (His future apostles and leaders) will be different and not function in the same manner as dictators who rule with control in this world, declaring that whoever among them wants to become a leader must first become a servant. Peter, the servant of Christ and eyewitness of many of His accounts, later stated in the book 1 Peter 5:2, as a forewarning and guidance to the leaders and spiritual guides of the church, to have a sincere care for God's people, not leading by cruelty, intimidation, oppression, or restriction, but enthusiastically and gladly, not disgracefully motivated by the compensation and proceeds from serving in the office, but willingly and freely, not by being a tyrant, a dictator, or an authoritarian, but as replicas and illustrations of Christian living.

Why am I saying this? Because over the past 25 years, I have seen the office of a pastor or leader severely altered and misrepresented and, unfortunately, I have seen many willingly embrace and invite this type of conduct. In most cases, in the end, the victims of this behavior are those usually excommunicated from the fellowship and left to survive on their own, battered and abused (spiritually). As they leave their ministries in hurt, new bodies, all willing and innocent, stand waiting to be taken advantage of. I'm also reminded about what Jesus told His disciples in the book of Matthew 23:4, that the Pharisees (the religious leaders of that day) were teachers of the devout law and His disciples were welcome to practice the law (which existed during that period of time), but were discouraged from living according to how they saw the modern leaders live because those leaders did not practice their own message. Furthermore, Jesus stated that those leaders squashed people under excruciating religious burdens, but never appeared committed to their own guidelines.

Finally, Jesus indicated that everything these religious leaders achieved, they broadcasted it in public in an effort to impress people; and, although these religious leaders appeared to be representatives of God, they were far from the reality of God. They looked religious, dressed religious, and acted religious but possessed no real spirituality. Jesus stated these thoughts to future apostles, admonishing them not to integrate these practices as leaders, though in today's society the outward performance by the Pharisees of old biblical times appears to be the essential principles many ministries have adopted.

The main ingredient that leads to spiritual abuse occurs when there is a deficiency of reading, studying, and researching God's Word for personal growth and knowledge. In the book of Luke 11:27-28, a woman in a crowd screamed out to Jesus, saying that His biological mother is considered great and blessed, only because she gave birth to Him (birth to Jesus). This is a prime example of how people exalt other people for unnecessary reasons. However, Jesus redirected the spotlight from humanity and returned the center of attention toward divinity by saying to this woman that those who are truly blessed are those who hear the Word of God and put it into practice. Oftentimes, people easily assume that every word spoken from the mouth of their leader is equivalent to Christ speaking Himself, and that's a formula for disaster. Christ is not instructing His leaders to become new messiahs in His stead, nor is Christ permitting leaders to become idols in the lives of His people.

To those leaders who do not practice this type of movement, nor allow God's people to exalt them high above measure, I say thank you, and thanks for knowing who you are in respect to who Christ is. Sadly, the reality is we have many superstar leaders who prowl, stalk, and prey on the weakness of others, especially those who are already experiencing some type of abuse, whether physical, spiritual, mental, or emotional.

However, the key to avoiding spiritual bitterness is to research every statement that's made by our leaders or anyone who's instructing you, including me, the author. Though leaders admonish God's people to study, what some really mean is: We are permitted to study God's Word as long as we perceive what we are studying in the same manner in which it is being preached or taught from the pulpit or platform. We must observe and interpret the passage of scriptures as we have been shown by our leader, but we are not allowed to study God's Word and come up with something completely different than what our leaders believe or think, because we'll then be guilty of having our own minds and be labeled as those who spread discord and possess critical spirits. But I am reminded about the passage of scripture found in the book of Acts 17:10-11, when the Apostle Paul preached to the people of Berea. These people were described as opened to hearing new concepts but were very careful to research and study every single word spoken by Paul concerning Christ, to make sure Paul was being truthful.

The word "search" in that passage of scripture means to examine or judge, to enquire into, to scrutinize, to sift, or to question in an investigation or interrogation sense. The people of Berea went back and examined every word spoken by Paul, but you will not find anywhere written in biblical history where Paul criticized these people for researching his message. In fact, it was Paul who admonished Timothy that by properly exploring and accurately associating and piecing together true biblical concepts, you can become a skilled and approved representative of God (without embarrassment) through personal study (2 Timothy 2:15).

It is the practice of many Christians to assume that the message disseminated on Sundays, and possibly other days during the week, is sufficient without the need for individual research. If we were given the option to eat just one meal per week and permitted to eat that meal on Sundays only, and being at the mercy of another man or woman who carries their own concepts of healthy eating habits, do you think we'll be physically fit or completely healthy? If not, then why do we imagine that our spiritual deficiency will be corrected by the poor spiritual habit of hearing God's Word only on Sundays for one or more hours for spiritual survival? To claim Christ as our personal savior means getting to know Him personally (a growing relationship) through His Word.

I am not suggesting that you ignore the message of your pastor or leader, but I am suggesting that you seek to become a student of God's Word by developing a unique relationship with God if you wish to avoid the spiritual pitfalls in Christianity. (No error or fault in Christ or His establishment, but we are imperfect people capable of earth-shattering mistakes.) The significance behind my communication is not to decrease the need for leadership in the body of Christ; this dialogue is presented to caution many believers not to substitute their leaders/leadership for God, and to remind many that numerous scriptural references warn us to beware of false prophets. (I will later discuss this in greater detail.)

I have seen thousands upon thousands of believers who have gone through the transformation of being the most treasured, appreciated, and respected person in Christian ministry, to being the most disrespected, ostracized, and discredited person due to a disagreement, controversy, or difference of opinion with their leaders. In an instant, the most beloved becomes the nearly forgotten. The saints integrate as a collective group to protect the guilty, being sympathetic toward the one at fault – usually a person of leadership (without even knowing or understanding all of the circumstances at hand), while isolating and disregarding the soreness of the victim or victims, usually the person who stood up to his/her abuser in the church, ministry, or organization.

We conduct ourselves in that manner because we have been trained to cover our leaders' sins (even if their sins destroy lives) while passing judgment against the innocent in an insensitive and unforgiving behavior. I am reminded about the letter the Apostle Paul wrote to the Corinthian church concerning going before the courts to settle disputes, stating that believers shouldn't file civil suits against other believers in the presence of those who do not share the same conscience of Christianity. Rather, these minor disputes should be easily handled from within the assembly (1 Corinthians 6:1-8).

Let me reemphasize the term "civil suits" and not "criminal cases." Paul strongly emphasized terms such as "minor disputes or small matters"; he also used terms such as "fault, wrong, and cheat." Paul said nothing about not going before the law/courts in criminal cases, and these criminal acts go unaccounted for in most ministries around the world. Leaders' raping men, women, and children, both boys and girls: one of many illegal acts that the church as a whole feels it's their obligation and responsibility to cover up and not expose. Paul also stated in 1 Timothy 1:8-10 (regarding the law of the land and not the law of Moses) that the law is a worthy tool if it's used suitably and properly, perceiving that the law is not made to reprimand righteous acts but designed to penalize those who are unlegislated and those who are willing to commit unlawful behavior, including those who sexually abuse mankind. For the record, I am a leader in the body of Christ and speak these things in retrospect to include myself.

I will never get comfortable and be at ease using verbiage such as, "You are my people," or "These are my people," when describing God's children, as if being a leader gives me the right to become your master in ownership. As a leader, I must continually endeavor to accomplish my calling in life for which I was predestined to perform, which is to teach the gospel of Christ with a sincere and pure heart, in a valiant effort to mature the body of Christ for the work of God's ministry while concurrently continuing to develop and retain my own relationship with my creator – for His glory and honor.

I cannot for one moment become idol in my responsibilities and begin incorporating strange practices and unfounded rituals in combination with my God-given purpose. (This underlying principle also includes living a productive life as a Christian.) King Solomon's report, found in the book of Ecclesiastics 8:11, states that when a transgression is not reprimanded promptly, people feel it is not dangerous to continue doing wrong. This passage of scripture was not written directly for sinners or saints, but it was written to educate all on why people choose to continue in unlawful activities until they are exposed, whether they are considered to be a saint or a sinner.

These seemingly small issues are those that should to be brought to light and addressed openly before the whole congregation in its infancy stages, prior to these problems mounting up and disrupting the functioning of the Christian establishment and devastating many lives. The emphasis of this book is to enlighten new, as well as mature, believers about the nature and practice of Christianity providing personal guidelines for proper conduct in Christian organizations. I also wrote this to remind leaders to revisit the roots of their foundation, making sure that it is continuously being constructed on Christ and founded in love, joy, peace, tolerance, kindness, righteousness, faith, humbleness, compassion, etc., rather than greed, self-focus, and self-indulgence.

Again, I am reminded about the passage of scriptures found in the book of St. John 5 and St. John 6, in which Jesus was speaking to the people about those who are true servants of God. As he performed miracles and fed multitudes of people in being a humble servant of God, this is what took place:

John 6:14-15:

"When the people saw him do this miraculous sign, they exclaimed, "Surely, he is the Prophet we have been expecting! When Jesus saw that they were ready to force Him to be their king, he slipped away into the hills by himself."

All too often, people are so influenced and captivated by miracles, signs, wonders, gifts of the spirit, and great works that they miss the entire purpose of these tools, which is to mature us as growing Christians. But, as you witnessed for yourself in the scriptures, people would rather anoint someone as their lord, master, or king, and be under someone else's tutelage and control, rather than seek God for themselves, living free from the supremacy of others.

Furthermore, when Jesus knew what the people were intending to do with him, he withdrew and hid himself, not allowing people to make him something he was not purposed for. Sadly, many leaders today observe this same trend, yet allow it for self-glorification, to be kinglike over God's people, crowned, anointed, and (literally) lifted above everyone else and carried to the podium.

Because God is omniscient (all knowing), he knew that one day the children of Israel would desire a human king to rule over them, as did all the other nations that encircled them. Prior to His people's desire for a king, found in the book of 1 Samuel, they were governed by mature leaders, judges, and elders, with the aid of prophets and prophetesses. God, knowing their thoughts, predestined their requests and had given His people an outline on the type of king he was permitting to rule over Israel.

In Deuteronomy 17:14-20, God stated that the king he desired for His people should be one of their own and not someone who they do not know or recognize (someone who they themselves observed to be honorable, honest, and who acted with integrity on a day-to-day basis). Their king should not be one who builds up large shelter of horses for himself, or sends his people to Egypt to purchase horses. In other words, God did not want the king of His people to emulate a nation that once controlled, abused, and destroyed them; neither did God want the king of His people to send them back to unify with a nation that he once delivered them from, or unify with a nation that once oppressed them.

The scripture goes on to state that God does not desire the king of His people to have many wives for himself; and he must not hoard large quantities of material wealth in silver and gold for himself; and he is required to get a copy of the instructions (laws) as they were given to His people – to read, learn, and obey (as a guideline for his own personal behavior). God continues to state that the king over His people must not become prideful and proceed as if he is beyond his fellow citizens.

If he, the king of his people, lives by the instructions that everyone else lives by, it will also prevent him from forgetting and turning away from God; and these instructions will guarantee that he and his offspring will reign for numerous generations in Israel. These things were spoken to the leaders of Israel decades preceding their request for a human king. It is amazing to observe in biblical history that God did not desire a king as a ruler of His people, to act as if he (or she – in reference to an authority figure) was greater than his/her own kind.

It is also amazing to examine that God did not desire a king to live by this prosperity doctrine that is so heavily taught and preached today, as if it's God's will for Christians is to become extremely wealthy in this life; and if we don't become wealthy, it is silently assumed that we missed God's purpose for our years of existence on this earth, or that we missed God's best in this life because we lacked the ability to gain assets and capital.

Christ even stated in Luke 12:15: Be on the alert, be cautious and be wary of materialism: for a man's life is not measured, deliberated, or calculated based on how much wealth you can own or how much material goods you can have or possess in this lifetime. (Sounds like the requirements that God had spoken about the king of His people as written in the book of Deuteronomy.)

There's absolutely nothing wrong with gaining wealth through hard work and fortune, but expanding our wealth based on manipulation of biblical principles is a whole different story. God's true emphasis about the kings of yesterday and His leaders/people of today is that we learned to support, love, respect, and appreciate each other in a unified way that brings glory to His name – in a way that represents him and His passion for humanity.

As we venture through this book together, please experience with me the mishaps of Christian behavior and the essential elements needed to restore and enjoy a prosperous relationship with Christ and others as we work together for greater intentions and reasons larger than us and greater in manner than just emphasis on a particular ministry or leader.

CHAPTER **1**

HEARING HIM

The Word of God has many attributes, and one of the numerous unique elements of this precious study guide is to observe and learn from the abundant examples that have already been laid for us to embrace or to avoid. The Apostle Paul informs the Corinthian church in Chapter 10 that the calamities that hindered the earlier believers of God were written as warnings and examples for us to learn as a lesson on how to avoid similar catastrophes. It is extremely important in these latter days that we pay very strict attention to our earlier paradigms.

The Bible tells us in the book of Isaiah 6:1-6 that in the year King Uzziah died, he then saw the Lord's glory. Isaiah later concluded that he was a sinful man with filthy lips, who lived among people with filthy lips. I'm sure many of us have read this passage of scripture, but concluded that we too have filthy lips, and then just moved on. But I would like for you to reexamine this particular lesson with me and explore the enormity of its factual implications.

King Uzziah (2 Chronicles 26), the ninth king of Judah, was anointed king at the age of 16 years old and served in his kingdom for 52 years, longer than any other king that preceded him. Uzziah was not like any other king before his time. He was exceptionally wise, virtuous, influential, and dominant in his youth, bringing his nation to a great time of affluence and prosperity, while defeating, subduing, and weakening the surrounding nations. The history of the Bible illustrates that Uzziah focused his attention on securing the defenses of both his capital and his country by building huge catapults that shot stones and arrows great distances. He also maintained a well-structured army suitable for war, and the Bible states that as long as Uzziah sought direction from the Lord, God prospered him – made him successful in his doings.

Isaiah was a prophet who was greatly influenced by the works and wisdom of this great king, to a point where it no longer mattered whether the king was doing good or evil – Isaiah faithfully followed him to the ends of the earth. Doesn't that sound familiar in today's society? The Bible continues to show us that King Uzziah's heart was lifted up in pride and that he no longer desired to be a moral king. He desired to be like some of his wicked colleagues and began doing what appeared right in his own eyes, justifying his conduct based on what God had done for him in previous years and his successes with the Lord.

As Uzziah begin catering to his own pleasures (excluding the Lord), many of his followers (to include God's prophet Isaiah) warranted his behavior by abiding with him, remaining steadfast and committed to him and not to the

God that King Uzziah served. As Uzziah's heart was lifted up in pride, so was his wisdom, his influence, and whatever he found himself devoted to performing. Remember, Uzziah served 52 years as the King of Judah, and my question is: How long did Isaiah follow him in his wrongdoings and prophesy things that agreed with the king's unlawful and wicked agenda? How long did Isaiah prophesy to God's people that the king was abiding in the will of God, affirming that the king's current actions were influenced by God and Godly directed? Bear in mind, it wasn't until the death of this influential king that Isaiah looked up and noticed the Lord instead of noticing Uzziah.

Please understand - It was through the lips of His prophets that God disseminated His Word. When Isaiah the prophet looked and saw the glory and pureness of the Lord, he immediately realized that he was a sinful man with _"contaminated lips"_ and lived among God's people with _"tainted lips"_, speaking things from his mouth that were not godly inspired or stimulated. After Isaiah's declaration of guilt, the angel of the Lord touched his mouth and told him that his iniquity and shame were taken away and that his sins were completely atoned for and forgiven. It took the death of a great king to get the prophet Isaiah to distinguish God in His true glory and splendor. It took the death of a great king to get the prophet Isaiah to realign his vision and focus on God and not man. If Isaiah got caught up in the pride of Uzziah's reign as king, which had shifted his center of attention away from the Lord, it is possible for us today to appear as if we are serving God, yet be too influenced and controlled by a man or a woman – whether they are doing good or evil – to even notice the difference.

It is so important that each one of us take the necessary time to examine our own lives to see who we are truly following. Yes, it is easy to say, "I'm following God or Christ," because we belong to a certain church or organization, or we affiliate ourselves with a leader or leaders who are well known in Christian ministry, but really, who are we truly following? Who are we listening to or being influenced by?

The writings in the book of Hebrews 1 tell us that in previous years and in a diversity of various ways, God had spoken to our ancestors through the prophets, but concludes that in these final days, he has spoken to us through His Son. So, if God has/is at present speaking through the message of His Son, Christ Jesus, my question is: What has the Son already spoken and what is he presently speaking?

That's so important for us to focus on and comprehend. Surely, some will say, "I can be the Son," or "You can be the Son," that the scripture is referencing; however, the scriptures go on to state and emphasize – "whom inherit all things, through whom also he created the worlds." That word "worlds" (in the Greek language pronounced "aion") means an unbroken age, a perpetuity of time, from generations to generations, not necessarily meaning different planets, but meaning to mark a period of time or generation. Now we know, as the children of God or the sons/daughters of God, that we have not yet inherited all things nor fashioned generations, so it is very important to note that the scripture states "that in these last days he is speaking to us through His Son" – Jesus Christ!

Now, let's focus on and observe Christianity as it is viewed today. Can we really articulate that Christ has spoken all these things that we are presently doing? Can we really declare that Christ has set in order all the things we have heard someone prophesied to us, to you, about your life, about your family, about your future, to include all of the mystical blessings that we wait and hope to receive?

Can we go back to the scriptures and trace whether or not the Son has verbally laid the foundation for us to obey the things that we are currently hearing – giving us the confidence to proceed and act upon? Have we identified and recognized how the Son truly speaks to His children? As Christians, we easily believe and act upon so many different things, but rarely consult with the Lord about His will or seek His confirmation, rather just believing and following everything we hear from somebody else and automatically accepting it as the Lord's voice.

This is a great danger and one of the most prominent mistakes found in biblical history.

As we discovered earlier, the prophet Isaiah, even as the Lord's prophet, fell into the trap of following everything he heard from his leader (without follow-up with God), being strongly influenced by the wisdom, gifts, talents, and the abilities of King Uzziah. When people give you a message declaring that it comes from God himself, do you immediately obey what someone has spoken to you or do you research every word to see whether or not it has come from God through His Son, whose voice is to be heard in these last days? It is imperative that we know what God has planned for our lives to avoid becoming a servant to another man's or woman's agenda.

God has ordained Christ to be His voice in these last days and has given us His message through His written word and speaks to our hearts through His written word – the history of our ancestors is clearly laid out before us – whether their actions were good or bad. The scriptures specifically point out to us that in times past, or in the previous years, he has spoken to us through His prophets – meaning that in the old biblical years, it was solely the prophets who carried the prophetic word from the Lord; but the scripture goes on to say that in these last days, he is speaking to us, not just through the prophets, but speaking to you and I through the voice of His Son.

Jesus stated,
"My sheep know who I am and when I speak they recognize my voice," and "You search the scriptures because you think they give you eternal life; but the scriptures point to me." (St. John 10: 1-5 and St. John 5:39, NLT)

This is the season to become mature Christians by affirming and confirming what you hear or have heard through the words of the Son through His written voice – the scriptures. This is the greatest key for avoiding the "bitterness of Christianity." It is time to rest from being tossed back and forth between every wind of doctrine (every new thing that's told to us). As the scriptures warn us – by the cunning and craftiness of men – whereby they position themselves in intervals, ready to deceive you and me.

That wind of doctrine can be from leaders (men/women) who are invited to your church, ministry, or organization – speaking to you as well as others – things that sound good to the ear, although those things spoken may not be biblically founded. Many may say, "My pastor would never allow that." In some cases, I can agree, but in most cases, when the focus is more on money instead of gaining more souls – it can and will happen, mistakenly and purposely.

Today, similar to physic readings, everyone has a "spoken word" for you; everyone is telling you what the Lord is saying, but nobody is examining whether or not that spoken word has come through His Son. As a leader in the ministry for many years, I have encountered a lot of guest speakers/ traveling ministers who came and went through various ministries and organizations, preaching and teaching unsupported and unfounded inspirational religious jargon; and, unfortunately, we as a whole did not properly discern or properly do our homework about the person who was selected to come and stand before God's people to teach.

And the results have been depressingly devastating. While we all expect everyone who stands on a platform with a microphone in hand, or with a wireless lapel mic, to be a positive/biblical Christian leader, many would instead harm God's people. The sad thing about that is, many leaders affirm those wicked and radical behaviors for the sake of personal gain, permitting these false teachers, ministers, preachers, pastors/prophets to come in and steal from the people of God by planting false statements (unbiblical reports) and empty promises for the sole idea of gaining wealth, fame, or fortune, to make a profit from the church through the unawareness of God's people.

I will be discussing the history and practices of false prophets later in this book, as it seems today that many have disregarded the teachings about false prophets, which is well documented through out biblical history and clearly referenced and long established, although it is rarely discussed in today's society, church, or organization. Now, how ironic is it that, one of the most attention-grabbing and educational topics is silenced? If any leader, including me, errs on the side of not researching the life and character of any guest speaker, that doesn't prohibit you/I from going back and referencing the scriptures to see if what was said is in agreement with what the Son has spoken and is now speaking.

We, as the people of God, have grown to accept anything our leaders accept and reject, everything our leaders reject without really consulting with the words of Christ. Do you know that both you and I will have to give a personal account to God on how we lived in this body on the earth, and how we strived to represent him? And our leader will not be standing next to us, coaching Christ on whether we should be received or rejected into eternal life.

This is not based on your initial confession of faith but is based on your initial confession *and* your continual exploration for God, laying down your own life for His. This is not founded solely on works or the number of mistakes we make, but based solely on your commitment to following and serving the Lord.

As the book of Romans Chapter 14 so eloquently states: "Each of us will give a personal report to God." When we die, we die alone and not with our leaders or anyone else. We should all recognize and thank God for those pastors and leaders who do not compromise who they are, those who humbly abide in their calling in which they were called (righteous servants of God), those whose hearts are toward serving and loving God, which would lead them toward serving and loving God's people.

But because the scriptures state that our righteousness is as filthy rags in comparison to the awesomeness of God's righteousness, and because of this, our true leaders still are not to be worshipped as Christ, for even they (our righteous leaders) are not those appointed to speak (from Heaven) in these last days. Yes, we as leaders are required by God to broadcast the message as a courier of the message, but not as the creator of the message. Many leaders today make it a requirement for us to support their personal opinions and lifestyles beyond the scope of Christ's written word.

Although we all are appointed to be ministers and servants of Christ (meaning our duty is to serve others, whether that means to serve others with what we know, as well as with what we have), we are designed to lead people to the one who has been designated and purposed to speak (removing the focus off us and placing it toward Christ). Why? Because we as humans are indeed capable of corruption (though many appear as if they never sin); our focus needs to be centered on the one who is incapable of error: Christ the Anointed. Christ is the one we should all be paying the most attention to through His already spoken word; he's the one we should all be focusing on. A lot of what we see today is such a disgrace to the kingdom of God because these actions don't mirror or reflect the power of His written word.

Also, a lot of what's observed today could facilitate us as individuals to escape spiritual tragedy and eliminate a great many mishaps in our Christian walk if we learn how to follow up and hear the one who has been appointed to speak in these last days. Jesus often hid himself away from people, secluded in the mountains, to pray. But, on one particular day, after a long a day of ministry with His disciples, Christ purposely took Peter, James, and John back with him to His familiar place of prayer in the mountains.

In the book of St. Luke 9, it tells us that when Peter woke up the next morning after a extensive day of ministry, he witnessed the magnificence of Christ (the splendor and grandeur of God's glory resonating on his Son); but Peter also recognized and identified two other interesting figures in conversation with Christ – Elijah and Moses. When Peter saw these great men with Christ, he did something most of us would have done and what most of us are doing now. The passage of scripture affirms that as these figures of Elijah and Moses were beginning to depart the scene, Peter stated, "Let me make THREE booths," or "three shelters as memorials."

I've often asked myself, now why would Peter be so anxious to build three shelters as memorials, knowing these figures cannot remain there? But as I read more about the purposes of booths, it broadened my knowledge. Booths were a temporary shelter, usually made of shrubs and tree branches, used to PROTECT cattle against the weather and to serve as a mark of respect to them.

So we can conclude that when Peter made this statement, he was aiming to protect those whom he strongly admired, and in creating monumental tributes to honor such esteemed men, Peter would be reminded every time he passed by the mountains and saw these booths, that he was in the company of great men. In fact, no implications in the scriptures leads us to believe that he even thought about making himself a booth, or making a booth for James and John, who were with him, but he offered to make these great men of God booths of memorials.

Now, please observe with me this point! Peter didn't just offer to make Christ a booth, but also a booth for Elijah and Moses as well. Peter included Christ, but he also included Elijah and Moses on the same pedestal with Christ. Elijah and Moses were great men of God who accomplished many remarkable things, and it was quite natural for Peter to include these men with Christ. Peter did not exclude Christ but included Christ, which tells us that Peter had great love and respect for the Son of God, just as much as he had for Elijah and Moses.

However, no matter what the case may have been, please notice how GOD responded to what Peter was thinking and had spoken. As we continue in the book of Luke 9:34, the scriptures go on to say that as Peter was observing these great men of faith standing with Christ, and speaking about the things he would like to do for them, communicating his thoughts, a cloud came down and overshadowed them (Peter, James, and John). They were overtaken with terror and stunned with fear as they entered into the cloud.

As Peter was saying "let's do something" for these great men of God, including Christ in his statements, the cloud came and impaired his vision. Peter, James, and John could no longer see theses men of God. Because of the intensity and thickness of the cloud, their vision was impaired, meaning their focus was blurred, distorted, and imprecise. God did not wait until after Peter completed building the booths for Christ, Elijah, and Moses, neither did God wait until after Peter was finished sharing his thoughts (because of his influence and the impact it had on the others around him, such as James and John). They were fearful because they could not see.

For many people today, a cloud has come and our vision is deeply impaired because our eyes are steadfast on people along with Christ. No, not excluding Christ, but including him along with the booths and monumental tributes we have built/made for many men and women of God on the same stage as Christ. There will be plenty who would deny this fact and reality, as well as others who would condemn this possibility and not be willing to accept their current state of mind because their vision may be grossly impaired, affected by the clouds of control and influence of others around them, leaving them visually damaged. Though we say we love God, though we say we put Christ first, our eyes are focused on other people on the same platform as God.

Whether these other people are doing great things for the Lord, or whether these other people are false prophets, our focus is steadfast on what we perceive in front of us or around us. We should not discount those who are faithful in Christian ministry, those who truly labor for the Lord, but we should not be building pedestals for them either. We should love, respect, and honor those who faithfully labor in Christian ministry, but we must exclusively praise and worship the God of salvation and the creator of our life.

Look what happened in the book of Luke 9:35, as Peter, James, and John were frightened by the cloud, they heard a distinctive and clear voice, which expressed to them:

"THIS IS MY SON (Christ), my dearly beloved; the one that I elected and preferred. Pay attention to and surrender to him with your full obedience."

Then, when the clouds cleared and the voice faded away, Peter, James, and John looked up and saw Jesus and JESUS ONLY, for he was there standing ALONE. God will not share His glory with another man or woman, whether they are striving to do good or evil. Build monuments in your hearts to the Lord (with praise and worship) and keep your focus and trust solely in/on Jesus. We should not abandon our trust in people or leaders, but it protects us when they fail us or when we fail them.

No matter who fails whom, there is one thing for certain: There's one thing you can count on. We can always depend on Jesus, for he has said he will never leave us nor forsake us and he's the only one who can make that promise and stand by it. The Apostle Peter understood this all to well (that God alone is worthy of all of our praise and that His glory should not be given to another or to human flesh).

As shown in the book of Acts 3, when he and the Apostle John ministered to the lame man at the gate called "Beautiful" and the Spirit of the Lord healed the lame man, the Christian brothers and sisters in Jerusalem gazed at Peter and John with astonishment, as if they themselves had performed this miracle in healing the lame man. However, the Apostle Peter noticed how the believers were admiring him and John for this act that was done. Peter responded in a remarkable way and in a means by which many leaders today would have not countered.

When Peter noticed all the attentive given to him and John by the Christian believers because of this act of healing, he immediately put an end to this behavior, as found in the book of Acts 3:12, and confronted the Christian believers. Peter stated:

"Why are you all acting so surprised and marveling at this, and why do you all continue staring at us as if we (Peter and John) by our own individual authority or devoutness made this man able to walk?"

Peter continued by also saying:
"This miracle that you all have observed was through and by the name of Jesus; it was by faith in His name this man whom you distinguish and are familiar with was made strong and well with soundness of body and mind."

If you continue reading in the book of Acts 3:11-19, Peter's statements to his fellow believers were so strong a reprimand that he informed them that their behavior was an act of ignorance and he demanded them to repent (to change their mindset and way of thinking). Peter was sharp with them in speech, because this issue of idolization is such a serious matter.

Unfortunately, many leaders today yearn and crave for that attention, to be looked upon with bewilderment and wonder when the Spirit of God performs a miracle of some sort, whether it be in the areas of healing, deliverance, or financial support. In fact, if we don't show some type of admiration toward some leaders, we will be chastened or reproved. Set your heart and affection toward God. As the psalmist sang in the book of Psalm 100:

"Get to know, comprehend, and remain mindful that the Lord is God and it is He who has made us and NOT we ourselves. We are HIS people and the sheep of HIS pasture; enter into His gates with thanksgiving and into His courts with praise; be thankful for him (acknowledging His goodness) and affectionately praise His name; for the Lord is good and His mercy and loving-kindness are perpetual and His faithfulness and truth is continuous toward all generations."

CHAPTER *2*

A BLESSING & A TRAGEDY: MY STORY

It's natural and very common to revisit and bring back those memories about when we first accepted Christ as our Lord and Savior. Oh, what a day of rejoicing it was: an overwhelming sensation of joy, a sense of freedom, and a brand-new association with others who had experienced this same transformation. What a good day that was as a brand-new Christian!

However, I would like for you to journey with me through my transformation of life: the pre-Christ days as well as the post-Christ occurrences, some thrilling and some not so glamorous; a blessing on one end of the spectrum and a tragedy on the other; a sense of feeling important and accepted, then the emotions of numbness and disturbance (being left behind like damaged goods). There is one true fact that Christian leaders can no longer ignore, conceal, or take lightly. That is, many Christians experience some type of physical, spiritual, emotional, or sexual abuse in Christian ministry (moreover in many other religious organizations).

Some are hurt so severely that without the proper nurturing and fostering to revitalize and heal their wounded souls, they will no longer desire the necessity to live for God, and their image of God will become corrupted by the imperfection and evil lusts of those who hold the office of a leader or a position in ministry. They feel abandoned and isolated from others around them because it seems that no one will take them seriously, or they know that others will not believe them, along with the added fear that those who serve in ministry with them will oppose them in support of their leader, even if their leader is the one at fault, the one who committed the wrong, or the one who is found guilty.

Abuse in Christian ministry (as well as other religious organizations) is real and common but rarely exposed, and should not be taken casually or for granted; furthermore, it is extremely important to identify and comfort those who have experienced some type of abuse in ministry to avoid those souls from becoming bitter with the Creator, and possibly remaining isolated and lost from the grace and mercy of God who is the invisible image of Christ. Not that God would ever detach himself for us; but it is our sin and shame that causes isolation and separation from God (Isaiah 59: 1-2).

I was born in Detroit, Michigan, and grew up in the Jeffrey Housing Projects. As long as I've been alive, I have known this place to be a notorious, crime-ridden housing area which plagued the downtown Detroit area and the entire city for nearly five decades. As history tells it, these housing projects were very popular in the 1950s; however, by the late 1960s, these once popular neighborhoods became a safe haven for drug lords and gangs, creating a neighborhood of extreme violence and high crime.

Many drug dealers chose this area as residents because it was effortless to transport drugs into Detroit's Cass Corridor, Skid Row, and the downtown area, being particular induced by the high volume of middle-class Caucasian men who traveled to the area in search of drugs or prostitutes.

The 1980s is where my story began, being cognizant of my environment, the people living in my surroundings, and my own conduct and behavior (being about nine years old at this time). As far back as I can remember, I've had to either fight for my life or run for my life in order to survive as a young man. In addition to being shot at and robbed at gunpoint, I've been an eyewitness to many being gunned down and have observed shootouts between rival gangs, including violence at my high school, Murray Wright High, which many called "Murder Wright" in those days (and this is in the '80s).

When I was nearly 11 years old, I remember a friend of mine calling me at home and asking me to come to his house to play. When I arrived at his house, I remember seeing my friend (the one who called me) and several of his friends running out of the house, screaming and yelling. When I walked into the house to see what was going on, I observed the brains of a young boy splattered on the chair and floor of the house.

I came to find out later they had been playing a game of Russian roulette. For those who are not familiar with Russian roulette, it is a game of chance where a player places a single round in a revolver, spins the cylinder, places the muzzle against his head, and pulls the trigger. This is the game my friend wanted me to come play at his house. I've watched people shoot heroin, snort cocaine, and smoke crack; it was nothing for me to see these things on a daily basis.

A Blessing & A Tragedy: My Story

There was even a time when I was hanging out with a friend in a crack house (a place where crack cocaine was bought, sold, and used) that was raided by the Detroit police. As they forced entry into this drug hub, I was thumped on my head with one of their baton sticks and was told to keep my eyes glued to the floor. As they questioned my purpose/business in that place (whether I was a drug dealer or an innocent bystander, at this time being about twelve years old), I responded to the police officers that my purpose for being there was to meet a friend and then go to a movie theater.

After hours of being scrutinized and hassled, they finally permitted me leave the house, which was the first and last time I ever hung with that particular friend, or hung in a drug habitation again. By the age of 15, I'd had around 25 close friends murdered and three times that number incarcerated. I remember another good friend of mine, at one point in time, who came to my house around midnight, trying to convince me to come with him to meet up with some girls he knew who lived on Fenkell Street, an area where we were forbidden by its rival/neighborhood gangs to hang out.

When I declined to go with him, he left my house around 1:30 a.m. Around 8:30 a.m. that same morning, we (me and another close friend) were crushed by the news that our good companion had been murdered, left for dead in the middle of the street as he was leaving some young lady's house. Boy! What a crushing blow and feeling that was for me at that time. I always believed, and became a living witness to this saying: "If you don't leave the environment – you become the environment." Many young men (including me) became victims and products of our own environment.

Although I was a very good athlete in three sports and could have easily played at the professional level in at least two of them (basketball and football), becoming something in life was a very low concern and priority. I managed my way through high school, being suspended (at the very minimum, once) at the elementary, middle, and high school levels for various reasons. But I vividly remember that at the age of 18 I was desperate for something new and original; something better than what I'd always seen and been accustomed to. I didn't know what I needed, I didn't know what I was searching for, but what I did know was – I desired more in life.

A close friend of mine and I became enemies over popularity (stirred up by materialism) to the point where one of us had to go to the grave. Being the youngest of three older sisters (on my mother's side of the family) and the oldest of three younger sisters (on my father's side of the family), for my father and mother were never married and me being the only male figure on both sides of the family; I knew I didn't want to die and that I had to do something different in life in order to survive it. I didn't know what to do at the time, being so confused with life, then all of a sudden an idea leaped into my mind. My cousin had recently joined the Navy and I began thinking "Maybe I can do that!"

Let me explain. I had absolute zero concept of the Navy, or any other branch of the military service. I mean, I didn't even know at the time that the U.S. Navy had anything to do with ships or water. All I knew was that I had to depart somewhere, anywhere, quickly. So, one day, I rose up early in the morning and walked to a military recruiter's office located in downtown Detroit. As often as I hung out downtown, I remembered seeing people wearing uniforms going in and out of a building, so I knew where the building was located, although I had no concept of a street address. As I entered the building, I remember walking into an office and inquiring about joining the military. The office I had wandered into was the U.S. Air Force.

Shortly thereafter, I was taking a test to join that branch of service. Unfortunately, I did not perform well enough on the exam to join the Air Force. However, I remember the recruiter telling me that my test scores were sufficient for me to enlist in the U.S Navy. I was introduced to and directed to work with a Navy recruiter. On July 7, 1989 (I can clearly recall this moment like it was yesterday), after I concluded my military physical examination, the Navy recruiter gave me the choice of joining the military and leaving for boot camp in about one year from then, or departing for boot camp in approximately five days. I chose to take off in the five days allotted. On July 12, 1989, I had joined the U.S. Navy, been sworn in, and was on my journey to something new.

In the interim, I went back home and informed my mother and sisters of the news, which was both bitter and sweet for them, as well as to others (my friends' parents), who had heard reports that I had joined the military. Many were both in high spirits and heartbroken to hear I was leaving; albeit, several were glad to see me disappear from my environment. A countless number of people, until this day, didn't think I would survive to see my 10th or 20th year high school class reunion, especially considering the path of life that I was living at that moment in time. So, there I was, escaping the concrete jungle (this is how my brick neighborhood was viewed – a tough place to grow up and live) and shipping off to U.S. Navy boot camp in 1989. Boy, what a culture shock that was for me. It was comparable to someone living in a hot climate of 100 degrees for 20 years and then the next day waking up to a temperature of -40 below zero. I mean, boot camp was a complete culture shock. But after everything I'd encountered in life, I knew above all things that I was going to give all I had to make it through boot camp.

Not only was I determined to succeed, I was confident I would accomplish this task, mainly because I was adamant about never returning to my old place of residence again, or at least not returning to that environment or those same set of circumstances that caused me to initially vacate. There was a period in boot camp in which I was deemed unqualified to continue with my original company (group of sailors to which I was assigned during the commencement of boot camp) due to my inability to adapt to this new culture and my inability to pass the academic segments of basic military training.

I was detached from my initial company and positioned in a holding unit (where you are basically in limbo – just training and progressing with no graduation or ending date in sight – until they feel you are ready to continue; when, at that point, you are placed with a new company/unit). I was in that indeterminate state for about two weeks, in addition to the general eight-week term of boot camp. There I learned and became equipped with handling military life. As the end of basic military training approached (thank the Lord), I strongly remember craving something new, and a hunger for more in life, but I didn't quite know what it was. I suspected it was just the idea of reuniting with my family and girlfriend (at the time), none of whom I'd seen since leaving for Navy boot camp.

After graduating from basic military training, I was given 15 days of leave to spend at home, prior to reporting to my first duty station in Norfolk, Virginia. Once I arrived back in Detroit, I spent some time with my mother, sisters, and other family members whom I'd dearly missed, then I caught up with my girlfriend to see how she was doing. After meeting with her, I still had a craving for something new, and being with her hadn't dissolved that feeling. Although allowed 15 days, I left Detroit in about five or six days and reported to my first duty station early.

Upon my arrival in Norfolk, Virginia, aboard the USS Vulcan AR-5, I was greeted by a young man who helped carry my sea bag and belongings to my sleeping quarters. This young man, from South Carolina, was cool to converse with, very down to earth, and happy about something, because he was very mellow and always smiling. Later that day, he asked me to come to church with him. It was on a Thursday night, December 7, 1989. I told him I would, but ended up meeting another guy from Alabama who reminded me of my past, so I hung out with him instead. Amazingly, something interesting happened as I was hanging out with the guy who reminded me of my past friends. All of a sudden, out of nowhere, I began feeling a consciousness of guilt because I didn't keep my word about going to visit this young man's church, as promised.

Keeping our word was a code of respect we (the fellas' in my neighborhood) practiced when I was living in the Jeffrey Housing Projects, because failure to do so could lead to some tragic consequences or a whole lot of fights. So I told myself, "Man, the next time I see this guy, I'm going to check out his church." As I spoke those words within myself, the guy who I'd selected to be with (who resembled my old company of friends) asked me, "Is everything all right with you, man?" I then responded, "Everything is fine. I was just pondering something."

At that point, I departed from this fellow; making the excuse that I needed to take care of some emergency business. As I was leaving the military gym (the place where we were located), I became hungry and walked toward McDonald's (located on the military base) to grab a bite to eat. As the street light turned red and I began crossing the street, I glanced over my left shoulder at the first car and noticed the guy who had invited me to church sitting in the front seat. It took less than a millisecond before we made eye contact. He rolled his window down and we began to chat. Before I knew it, I was in the car with him heading to a men's gathering at his church that evening of Tuesday, December 12, 1989, which would be a night that changed my life forever. So, as I entered the church building, I met a lot of cool men who were lively, down to earth, and quite comical. That kept me very interested in understanding why these guys were fun to be around.

My previous perception of what I called "church people" instantly changed. I had always thought people who attended church were nerds, square (isolated from pleasure), and boring. One thing I knew for sure. If I began hanging out with these guys, I might be able to stay out of trouble. Later that same night, all the men were asked to move toward and assemble in the sanctuary, where they were beginning to have a devotion of some sort.

While I was standing in attendance and listening, God began working on my heart. Then the pastor began teaching about the grace and mercy of God, which indeed grabbed my attention. My mind began to reminisce on all the times I had longed for something new. I asked myself "Could this be it? Could this be what I was yearning for?" At that moment, my eyes were opened toward God's love for me, and I desired this thing called "Christianity." Later that night, I chose to receive Jesus Christ into my heart as my Lord and Savior and then was baptized. I didn't have a clue as to what I was doing, nor did I comprehend what I was committing myself to.

One thing for sure, I recognized that I was making a change for the better, and that "something new" fixation I'd been craving was a relationship with Jesus Christ in communion with God. For the first time in my entire life, I understood the meaning of peace – not necessarily the peace in this world, but peace in my heart – no more having to look over my shoulder in hope of being alive to witness the next day. Although I received the free gift of salvation, I also inherited the error of humanity in Christian ministry, or any religious organization (by default), which I would become acquainted with in years to come. This was the beginning of my fluctuant journey.

The Bible states in the book of Proverbs 27:7:
"A person who is full refuses honey; but even bitter food tastes sweet to the hungry."

And, boy, new Christians accept a lot of things as sweet to eat (because of their newly discovered hunger and thirst after righteousness), although it's bitter food (things that are not biblically sound, but rather humanly conspired).

Many Christians, both mature and babes, assume every deed that's done in response to their leader's request is good and blessed by God, regardless of the action committed, whether sweet or sour. And many vinegary or acidic activities take place right in the house of God in silence, such as sexual immorality and manipulation, physical assault and abuse, mental and emotional empowerment, or controlling and dominating tactics that are used to gain supremacy over the lives of God's people – and social abuse, in which your connection with people or association with other believers in ministry is entirely centered around your ability to follow the restricted protocol and social order of the church, organization, ministry, and minister, regardless of your relationship with Christ.

I'm not so much concerned or troubled with the actions of new believers in ministry, or babes in Christ (because they may not understand all the fine points about Christianity as they demonstrate more zeal than knowledge during the conception period of their faith), but I am referring to the boundless number of (supposedly) mature Christians and ministries.

Although all leaders do not conduct themselves in disturbing activities, many who embrace the titles of bishop, apostle, prophet, pastor, evangelist, or teacher are blameworthy of these alarming tragedies (due to their own immaturity in Christian behavior and their uncontrolled lusts, extremely gifted and charismatic but still unlearned and inexperienced), all in the name of the Lord.

This discussion is not at all aimed at targeting people who fall short to sin, because we all have free access, through Christ, to seek God for repentance. I am speaking about the daily participation and practice of numerous immoral acts executed with people in the body of Christ or in the general public sector. Not only are these deeds lived out consciously and deliberately, but they have convinced themselves and the people who support them, that they are not in violation of any misconduct; embracing self-denial based on the fact that God has not immediately judged or punished them for their corrupt conduct.

Therefore, as a substitute for God's people condemning such actions (not the person, but rather the behavior), they conceal these practices and continue supporting and praising their leaders under the conviction and belief that they are not obligated to righteously judge dreadful behavior, even if the leader is practicing wrongdoing.

Although I agree that we, through human nature, should not judge others (in the manner of eternal condemnation and disapproval) based on our own personal sensitivities, the Bible has given us the authority to judge (in the manner of being an arbitrator) according to the already proven and purified Word of God as affirmed in the book of St. John 7:24. God's spoken and written word serves as the ultimate referee and umpire for regulating acceptable and unacceptable behavior.

No human being, no matter what title they may hold in this world, has the authority to disregard the restrictions, limitations, and freedoms of the established Word of God. As I continue with my story, I implore you to recognize that my dialogue is more from a realistic point of view than a creative imagination. Many have served as the victims or perpetrators of abuse in ministry, as well as many who have stood idly by and ignored the cries of those being victimized. Whatever the case may be, we can no longer remain voiceless and overlook these sinful practices.

Your silence will be mistaken as consent rather than disapproval. While speaking in opposition toward certain leaders and ministries carries consequences, and you will be viewed as being insubordinate, rebellious, and immediately isolated and cut off from the people you serve with in fellowship/ministry, your spoken voice can change the course and nature of mistreatment in ministry while sparing others from the horrific experience of spiritual exploitation. I truly believe that without a struggle, there can be no progress, and without adversity there can be no triumph or success. I also believe that if you don't stand for something, you will stand for nothing, or fall for anything and everything.

So, in my first ministry (which I'll call FCFC), we were taught that communication was important to the Lord, and that God would have us communicate every thought we were thinking and every action we were planning in every setting of our lives, forwarding that information to the pastor/ministry or to the leaders/powers that be (for the purpose of control and the authority to manipulate). FCFC had unpaid staff members who worked for the ministry (for many years) 24 hours a day (literally). There was a team of staff members (on which I served) who were trained in how to answer the ministry's phones and relay all messages accordingly. For anything this ministry required of us or inspired us to perform, we were always given scripture references, references out of context from the original biblical meaning (as now I've been enlightened to understand).

Many of us (young men and women), as well as many of you, were blinded by the excitement of salvation, which made everything appear so innocent, lovable, and praiseworthy. FCFC was a ministry that was open seven days a week (six days were built around fellowship, training, and bible study for single men and, typically, Sundays were set aside for morning and evening worship services).

We were trained to believe that the importance of fellowship (seven days a week) would protect us from sinning and keep us from neglecting the assembling of ourselves together, as stated in the book of Hebrews 10:2, so we literally went beyond the proper interpretation of that scripture reference. In the late 1980s, cellular phone ownership and users were typically business proprietors, those who were wealthy, or those who could afford them. And, yes, even in the late '80s and early '90s, pay phone usage was, for the most part, the largest part of telephone communication.

We were living on board a naval ship, and the pay phones that all sailors used were usually at the end of the docks, which could easily take you 10 to 15 minutes from any location on board your ship just to get to those pay phones at the end of the pier, not counting the length of time used on the phone, and then returning to your ship. My communication (as well as many others) was so extreme (as we were taught) that at the end of my workday, I would literally leave my ship (still nasty and not clean after a hard day at work) and walk 10 to 15 minutes to get to a pay phone. If one wasn't available, I waited until one became available, then called the church and relayed these magical words, "I'm off work and getting cleaned up," just to have someone waiting to pick me up at the end of the pier to take me and many other men to the church for fellowship and ministry, and to keep us from being contaminated by the world. So, immediately after I'd contacted the church, I walked 10 to 15 minutes back to the ship to get cleaned up and ready for men's fellowship. (This was a daily occurrence for me for countless years.)

In addition, after getting cleaned up, if my ride wasn't waiting at the end of the pier when I arrived, I called the church again to communicate that I was ready and waiting. Also, there were many others brothers in Christ affiliated with the ministry in the U.S. Navy, and I was usually tasked (as the big brother) with going to the other ships to make sure the newer and younger Christians were ready and willing to participate in the seven-days-a-week ministry to be nourished and enlightened by the Lord. I practiced this behavior for a least seven consecutive years, day in and day out, for it was the older Christians' entitlement to make sure the younger Christians did not spend their time in this carnal world with its wicked practices, as we were taught. Because, as we had always stated, "There's no other place you rather be than in the house of the Lord, right?"

We believed that if you were part of FCFC ministries, you were in the will of God, the light of God, and the salvation of the Lord; and if you ever left this ministry; you would be lost from God's salvation for eternity and end up in hell because you did not abide in the calling for which you were placed by God to support in ministry. This is what we were taught then and this doctrine and mindset, believe it or not, is still being taught and practiced today in many ministries, for the sake of power and control over the lives of God's peoples, as if the Spirit of God is incapable of keeping his people safe.

If Christ himself is unqualified to protect and keep His chosen people secure no matter where they are (hypothetically jesting with serious motives), then we are all doomed and there is no church, ministry, organization, or leaders, such as, bishops, pastors, prophets, popes, or anyone qualified enough to deliver us out of harm's way.

We are and have been created for the glory and purpose of God through the crucifixion and resurrection of Christ, and established by the comfort of the Holy Spirit. I am fully acquainted with the importance of ministry with the assembly of other believers, but this concept of "Christian fellowship" is nothing more than a place to hang out, or a social club, if we, as individuals, do not grasp the true significance of fellowship, which is to establish our own personal walk with the Lord (by prayer, through the obedience of His Word, and with pleasure).

Our partnership should be with other believers who share those same pure motives and practices, although we may have different opinions and experiences with possible disagreements (and these attributes are what make the body of Christ much stronger and healthier), and though we have different backgrounds in intellect, environment, and ethnicities, we can still work as a "collective unit" in unity as witnesses and examples of Jesus Christ. If there is a ministry that agrees on every single subject, single matter, and single thing, please beware, be alert, and be on guard, because that is a recipe for an unhealthy environment (a cult, similar to what I was a part of). When the Apostle Paul encouraged the church in Ephesus to be of *"one mind and one accord,"* that was not an indictment toward those with differences.

Despite our many differences, God's people are encouraged to have similarity and congruency in our relationship with Christ and our purpose together in the body of Christ, which is to unify for a greater cause, a reason much bigger than our own personal accomplishments and achievements. As I have heard in the past, going to church doesn't automatically make you saved or become a mature Christian, no more than going to McDonald's makes you automatically the CEO or part owner of the corporation.

There is a misconception with believers in thinking that affiliation with a particular "popular leader or ministry" is equivalent to Christ's call for His people and His desire for us to be personally acquainted and familiar with His "Word" and "Voice" through biblical literature and personal connection. There are those who accept and believe that the word of their leader(s) IS INDEED the word and voice of the Lord, which is another recipe for catastrophe.

As I have communicated many times, as an ordained leader and teacher, when I suggest, impart, or admonish you or anyone about a particular subject or topic of scripture, I always encourage my listeners to go back and research what is taught/preached for themselves for two meticulous reasons: 1) to broaden their knowledge of God about the subject, and 2) to make sure the things spoken to them are accurate and sound, because the Bible warns us that there are many false prophets and teachers in the world. Which means these false representations of Christianity live within our communities, ours neighborhoods, and, sadly, in our churches, ministries, and organizations. My first ministry, FCFC, which I was affiliated with, and before you accurately judge it or consider it a "cult," was a nondenominational ministry. We understood and strongly believed that we were nothing like a "Jim Jones" or "David Koresh" type of ministry. Many of us over exaggerated our communication to this ministry to the point that we couldn't or wouldn't even go to a fast food restaurant without the permission of the ministry or a least without informing the pastor or a staff member.

At all times, the ministry was fully informed of our whereabouts and, boy, did we ever feel proud that we were pleasing the Lord as we were taught. Not only did we communicate to this extreme but we were also taught to give our money and income as the first response of our salvation with God, as if money is the link and key to our salvation. Neglecting or not giving the dollar bill (money in general) is as wicked as someone who chooses to live in sin, or someone rejecting the salvation of Christ.

I recently heard a pastor state before his congregation (me being in the audience) that tithing is your first response to true repentance and obedience to Christ, not repentance from sin, not the acceptance of your salvation, not prayer, not living for God, not spreading the good news of Jesus Christ, but the giving your money is your first response to obedience. Money is a tool which, if used properly, assists the poor and needy and furthers the spreading of the Gospel of Christ, not building personal kingdoms on earth, which we strongly observe in this day and time.

With all respect, I humbly encourage everyone to get a copy of my book entitled: "*The Emancipation of Tithing*", which could be obtain directly from Enlightenment Publishing LLC website (this information is located in the front of the book). In it, I teach in great detail and with spiritual intensity about tithing and freewill offerings. (Today people rarely hear a message taught about "freewill giving.") In FCFC, we were told to pay tithes, but were never taught about the history of tithing. Many of us gave 50% or more to this ministry for numerous years. After all, what could we achieve with this money, other than to enjoy it for the pleasures of our own flesh and our own wicked desires (as taught); furthermore, it belonged to the Lord anyway and all we were doing was giving it back to him. Sound familiar?

Those were the implications and subliminal messages we heard preached. No one ever objected to the way we gave, or educated us to understand what we were doing with our finances. Furthermore, many of us never saw a tax return refund as long as we were part of the ministry. For some, it was six years; for me and others, it was seven to eight years; and for others, it was more years than I wish to express or remember. Our tax return refunds, we were told, would be used for the sake of "God's ministry" and for the benefit of the "Bishop's defense fund," which I will further explain later.

The dynamics of my message are not designed to tear down the churches of God and disgrace the Lord, or give any an excuse not to surrender their hearts and lives wholeheartedly to the service of the Lord; however, my communication is intended to educate, expose, and enlighten, those who will hear, about the downside of ministry, and how to overcome and avoid the bitterness of Christianity so we can serve the Lord with pure hands and a clean heart. FCFC had four main branches located in Orlando, FL, Waukegan, IL, Norfolk, VA, and San Diego, CA. After the naval (boot camp) base closed in Orlando, along with some personal issues between the pastor in Orlando and the bishop in Waukegan, the church in Orlando closed its doors. (Smaller fellowships associated with this ministry were located in other parts of the world due to military men who traveled worldwide.)

The main churches were strategically positioned near the naval bases as that was the ministry's foremost goal; to recruit single military men in all three locations. We praised ourselves and our branches of ministry because of the number of military men we were able to win to the Lord: a minimum of at least 100 single men, if not more, serving in each location. Soon after, the churches began their single men's ministry crusade. Although the pastors were married, the ministries functioned off the sweat and controlled labor of the single men in the ministry. In all three branches, one by one, every man would eventually sit with the leadership of the church and be asked, if not heavily persuaded and recruited, to make a vow to God not to marry, but to remain single for the rest of their lives for the sole purpose of serving the ministry. Oftentimes, the main emphasis of scripture, that was used out of context to convince and persuade many men to commit to the churches' wicked deeds, was what Jesus stated in the book of Matthew 19:12:

"Some are born as eunuchs, some have been made eunuchs by others, and some choose not to marry for the sake of the Kingdom of Heaven. Let anyone accept this who can."

And a countless number of men fell into the trap of committing themselves as eunuchs for the sake of this ministry and the personal pleasures of the bishop. Yes, I was approached, and after being tirelessly pressured, I told the leadership that it would be hard for me to carry out because I'd had girlfriends prior to being saved in this ministry and that I still desired female companionship and planned to marry one day.

Then, for the moment, my recruitment to eunuchship ceased, but the abuse was just beginning. Those of us who had bravely refused to become male slaves for the personal gratification of the ministry were required to find a spouse in this ministry and this ministry alone – outsiders were heavily criticized (whether saved or not). If you had a girlfriend prior to joining the ministry, or if you met someone outside of this branch of ministry, this person must be willing to join the ministry – there were no negotiations or exceptions. There was a time I informed my pastor that I had interest in a saved woman in Detroit (who is now my wife), and the pastor required me to see if I could get this friend of interest to come and visit the ministry in hopes that she would instantly join and relocate to Virginia.

So, I asked my friend from Detroit to come visit the ministry and paid her expenses. To her surprise, for the seven days she was in Virginia, she only saw me three times: once when I picked her up from the Greyhound bus station, once on Sunday morning, then once more on her way to the bus station heading back to Detroit. (The whole time she was in Virginia, she stayed with some of the single women in the ministry. We spent no time together.)

My future wife (prior to our marriage) informed me months later that she didn't like the ministry and that my pastor, who was unfamiliar with her, tried to pressure her into moving to Virginia without delay. She told me in the early '90s that if she and I were to ever get married, it would not be in this ministry (under this pastor or leadership). From that point on – there was a three- to five- year period where we had absolutely no communication with each other. However, in later years, after I departed from the ministry, we were reunited and married in 1997.

This year, in 2014, will be our seventeenth wedding anniversary. The single women in FCFC ministry were a small group and were not recruited as the single men were. Although military women were part of the ministry, more women were recruited locally then from the military bases. When the single men and single women met up on Sunday mornings prior to the worship service, the single men were on one side of the room while the single women were on the other side, chatting.

Many people who visited the church found this practice strange, but we were ready to defend our actions and usually told people that this was intended to keep us from lusting and to keep us focused on Christ. I'm still laughing today. What a joke! One of the real reasons was to keep those men who had committed to living their lives as eunuchs from desiring a wife, and for the pleasures of the bishop when he visited.

The married families who were part of the ministry were nonexistent or ignored, unless the married men agreed to spend more time with the church and less time with their wives/families as their way of illustrating their commitment to the Lord and to the church. Many complied (to their shame) to the restrictions and wishes of the ministry.

The single men were often discouraged from taking a vacation and going home to visit their families; and if they were to take vacation, many were strongly encouraged to stay in Norfolk, spending time running errands for the church. The rationale used to dishearten men from taking vacations and going home to visit family was that by doing so they might be misled by family members or others to turn away from serving the Lord and the ministry. If you were esteemed as a mature Christian in the Lord (usually after years of being brainwashed by the techniques of the ministry and well equipped to resist outside sway), you were permitted to go home, as long as you called the church on a daily basis to communicate your activities and give testimony as to how things were going while you were away from the ministry.

It was the ministry (100% of the time) that provided transportation to and from the airport. Yes, we were taught that if you ever left the church/ministry, Hell would be your final destination, because when God calls you to a ministry, you cannot depart unless God informs the pastor. Of course, the pastor always said, "The Lord didn't release you to leave." And those who eventually departed from the ministry were either: barred/banished due to noncompliance, transferred to another branch in the same ministry or they simple got tired of the abuse and departed.

In all three locations, California, Virginia, and Illinois, the ministry collected enough money to purchase apartment complexes within a half-mile radius or less from the ministry. (At one point there was an apartment complex located directly behind the church.) The apartment complexes were used to house the single civilian men. These single men were usually those who had separated or retired from military service, and instead of going back home (the last place they lived prior to joining the military), many resided in these apartments and obligated themselves solely for the provisions of the ministry, as a way of exhibiting their personal commitment to God.

The civilian men who were employed were obligated to surrender their entire paychecks and pool all their money together. The ministry collected the money then provided those men their desired necessities. (These finances were also utilized to compensate all the church's personal and business expenses.) If the civilian men requested new clothes, new shoes, haircuts, work uniforms, or anything, they had to first demonstrate a legitimate need for these things. Then, on Saturday mornings, those who had justifiable requests were duty-bound to write their names on several lists which were typically posted in the church's fellowship hall throughout the week.

These lists were reviewed on Fridays by leadership, and failure to get your name on any one of those lists could prolong your desired request for another week. Those men who had similar necessities rode together in one vehicle (usually a church van) and shopped at the same department store. If that particular store did not have the desired item in stock, then they usually had to wait another week before they ventured out again into the uncultivated society (they were not permitted to continue shopping from one store to the next). Although we single military men had the convenience to go to our military exchanges (military stores) on base anytime during the week after work, we opted not to use that allotted time, freely given to us without restraint. Rather, we waited until Saturdays and joined the other civilian brothers in the ministry.

The ministry was open seven days a week. Usually, we had Bible study or some type of men's gathering scheduled six days out of the week. The civilian men were not permitted to go outside of the ministry to eat food, which was made available seven days a week by the church cook. Although there were restaurants in the vicinity of the area, even directly across the street, you were not allowed to go and spend the church's funds that you personally labored for and earned all week. (If, by chance, the civilian men worked a very late shift and there was no food available for them to eat at the church, then and only then were they allowed to eat from a restaurant with the pastor's permission of course.) In addition, there were scarce times we did eat at a restaurant, and that was when the bishop came to visit the branch in Norfolk to inspire the single's men ministry.

We were so proud that we were fulfilling the scripture found in the book of Acts 2:44-47:

"...all the believers met together in one place and shared everything they had and have all things in common; they sold their property and possessions and shared the money with those in need."

In reality, we were not liberally unified for a common purpose in Christ as much as we were in harmony and fused together under the control of the pastor's psyche – puppets on the strings of our puppet master. During this time in ministry, though I was not committed to the single men's agenda in terms of my priority of marriage, I was considered a general, elite leader in the organization. A gifted young man – gifted in wisdom and knowledge, skilled with my hands and feet, committed to the origin of the church and ministry, as well as to the Lord – used tremendously and heavily in connection with the leadership (as were many of the single men – gifted, talented, and worn).

I often traveled with the leaders, whether by plane or car, to serve and assist them and their families – whether in Illinois or Virginia (never visited the ministry in California). So I was wholly exposed to the elements of the ministry, recognized for my accomplishments, and equipped to operate in the areas of grooming other leaders. I was that hungry soul eating every bitter thing, thinking that it was sweet and good to consume.

As I was more privy to the functioning of the ministry and leadership, I began observing immoral practices concealed behind closed doors, and although there were various scandalous and disturbing activities carried out, many of us were deceived and spiritually blinded by the voices of those in leadership (many of those who served as leaders were scripturally persuasive and gifted in the art of deception). The senior pastor of all the FCFC ministries was a bishop who pastored the branch located in

Waukegan, Illinois. In the mid-1990s, he was finally convicted of aggravated criminal sexual abuse, criminal sexual assault, and child pornography. (Prior to his conviction, these allegations consistently surfaced about him and the ministry for more than 30 years, since 1965.) He later died while incarcerated.

For countless years, the leadership of this ministry constantly and continually covered up and lied about the bishop's sexual appetites and his influential ability to force single young men to have sex with him. As long as I can remember, whenever these allegations about our bishop surfaced in all the branches of ministry, we vigorously denied all accusations. Though there were men who were part of these sexual encounters, they too, with determination, denied the negative remarks/comments under the guile of deception and self-embarrassment.

Prior to the bishop being indicted and imprisoned, I not only met him, but was recognized by him as a strong part and leader in the ministry (let alone being honored by him, convening with him in person was equivalent to meeting the Pope or your favorite musical artist). There had been scores of men (of all ages) who had claimed for numerous years that our bishop in Waukegan had molested and raped them (including many boys who were minors). I used to ask myself, "But how can this be, for I have been with/around the bishop a lot and he never approached me in any harmful way?" Besides, the bishop was an older Caucasian man who was married to a woman and had been married for more than 46 years. There was a time I was with the bishop in his automobile (visiting the ministry) and he was on his speakerphone, built into his car, conversing with one of the newer members in the ministry.

He asked the young man whether or not he had been smoking cigarettes. When the young man replied " no", the bishop told him that not only was he being dishonest, but he named the kind of cigarettes he was smoking, the number of cigarettes he smoked, and gave him the precise number of cigarettes remaining in the packet (the bishop had the gift of discernment).

Nonetheless, as people departed the ministry, one by one, many continued to vocalize their encounters with the bishop and his sexual practices.

Albeit, the more we heard these rumors, in all the branches and locations of ministries, the more we denounced these rumors as being false. The bishop often visited the other locations of ministry to defend himself and persuade the single men of his innocence. When he visited the branch in Norfolk, Virginia, he often requested to converse with me one-on-one, no matter where I was; and although I felt I offered a strong source of leadership to him and the ministry, his purpose for me went much farther than what I anticipated. All of a sudden, at the peak of my religious fame – *Boom* – all the rumors I had heard and violently denied came to illumination and exposure. One day, as I was visiting the ministry in Waukegan, I was beckoned to the ministry's main office and told that the bishop requested my presence at his home office located on Old Plain Road in Illinois. My pastor at the time, the pastor in FCFC Norfolk, who I accompanied to Illinois, had been tasked with picking me up from the church office and bringing to me to the bishop's home office.

His home office was operated and managed by all single men (all free labor) and used as the corporate headquarters for all communication and correspondence purposes. So, at any given moment, there could easily be a minimum of 15 to 25 men at the bishop's home office (which was considered the corporate headquarters) at all times. I remember vibrantly the excitement I felt; being summoned to meet the bishop once more. I could not get there fast enough to answer his call and to fulfill my appointed mission/call of duty.

My senior pastor dropped me off at the back entrance of the home office, and then continued his journey in another direction. When I walked into the home office, I was greeted by at least a dozen men who were working tirelessly in handling all the mail and correspondence for all the ministries (very busy place in all perspectives). Within 10 minutes of my arrival, I was subpoenaed to the bishop's personal office located on the second floor of the home.

Before I continue, let me express that when I connected with the bishop, whether in person or over the phone, more than 20 times he steered the conversation in the direction of my desire to be married and talked about understanding my sexual preference for women and how God was going to help me overcome the temptations of wanting to be with a woman until I was married. (At the time, I just took it as him being a spiritual father, as that was his job, for he was plain and blunt in speech.)

So, after being summoned to his office, I gingerly sat in the chair across from him, and he began talking about my sexual interest in women, and solicited from me how I was doing in that area. After informing him that I was doing well, and though I would like to be with a woman, I wasn't too stressed or concerned about my relationships with women or any of the sisters in the ministry.

As we continued with our dialogue, he talked about a method used for years to overcome the temptation of sex with women, without the temptation of masturbation, saying that God would rather have you to do this (the thing he was about to advise me), rather than to masturbate and spill your seed – although he acknowledged that masturbation was better than committing fornication/adultery with a woman. So I asked, "Do what?" and he replied, "Do this," then he asked me to follow him to the main room located in another area on the same floor of the home.

When he opened the French doors of that room, I observed more than a dozen men having sex with each other. The bishop immediately pulled off his clothes and joined in with those men. He invited me to participate with them when I became comfortable in taking part, beckoning me to join in, as it would eventually become natural for me to perform. He also told me that what they were doing wasn't what I was thinking – this was just a way for the men to get over their craving for a woman and to protect them from lusting.

The sad thing is that although I did not commit or participate, I believed his words and was persuaded by his speech, again contemplating within myself, "How could he be lying? He is married to a woman, after all, and how could the Lord give him these gifts if he was being deceptive?" I strongly debated as whether or not I should join in – many of the men I seen were leaders of renown and reputation—ministry wise.

With hesitation and intense nervousness, I took a few steps back, closed the door to the room they were in, went downstairs, and joined in conversation with the men on the first floor. Although I acted as if nothing had happened, I was torn apart emotionally and mentally. I mean – just ripped asunder spiritually. The other men, though accustomed to what was taking place upstairs, were consciously seared, pretending everything was normal. Eventually, my pastor from the location in Norfolk (the bishop's son in law) returned to pick me up from the bishop's home office. (He greeted me with a smile.)

Let me interrupt my train of thought for a moment by affirming:

Annually, during my physical examination, I am checked for prostate cancer which is usually common in older men; especially African American men. The first time my doctor lubricated his finger and stuck it in my rectum, I nearly hit my head on the ceiling because that was extremely uncomfortable; and all I can say after my checkup was "God I thank you for allowing me not to experience any form of physical sexual abuse; although I experienced an ample amount of psychological cruelty.

Later, I was contacted by the bishop over the telephone, and for many years to come, he influentially inspired me to believe that what I had seen taking place in Waukegan, Illinois, were not acts of homosexuality (because he did not have lust or love in his heart for these other men). However, as much as I wanted to please and impress the bishop, I informed him that I did not participate with them because I felt uneasy and panicky. (I made this statement to him in an appealing way that made me appear in the wrong, and him materialize in an acceptable behavior to justify his immoral actions – for I feared the bishop and his power to influence and control everyone in the ministry.)

The bishop told me he understood where I was coming from and excused my nonparticipation, and then he asked me not to broadcast what I observed. He continually assured me his attempts were always in the best interest of all the men, as it was his "spiritual calling" to nurture and mentor those men who had committed to the ministry of eunuchship as a way to help these men overcome their addiction of women.

Again, I believed every word that came from his mouth, blinded by deception due to his spiritual gifts and cunningness. And, although I had been personally exposed to the bishop's folly and wickedness, for a short time I continued to go along with the program and defended his innocence. Again, in the mid-1990s he was incarcerated because several youths were strong, brave, and wise enough to reveal the bishop's lawlessness, their encounters with him, and the ministry, to the authorities.

As I later came to find out, the bishop's criminal history and sexual involvement with minors were well documented since the 1970s. When the bishop was incarcerated, the ministries nationwide banded together and came up with the idea to use the single men's tax refunds to fund the bishop's defense lawyers, known as the "Defense Fund." So, for the life and span of your time connected with this ministry, although you signed your tax returns, you never saw a refund (out of sight, out of mind, and not concerned).

Your tax documents were turned over to the church's accountant who filed them for you and deposited your refund electronically into the church's central banking account. Since my departure from the ministry in 1995-96, I have encountered a number of men who also left the ministry; however, many of them are damaged for life, incapable of forgiveness, and with little to no healing process while many struggle to function as a man.

And from this time forward (due to my knowledge of what was occurring behind closed doors) in the ministry, I became angrier and more mischievous, more unsettled, and more prideful in my conduct and behavior. To keep me from sharing with others or confessing what I knew about the bishop and the ministry, the bishop indirectly encouraged me and influenced a relationship between me and his granddaughter (her father being my pastor in Norfolk, and my pastor being a son-in-law to the bishop).

I came to find out that my pastor, along with another pastor in Waukegan, had been mysteriously married off to the bishop's two daughters. This relationship in its infancy stages (between me and his granddaughter) seemed pure, but later became the commencement of my dreadful downward spiral in the ministry. My pastor's daughter and I became inseparable, and in the fellowship hall on Sunday mornings, instead of the men being on one side of the room and the women on the other, she and I were together. Many knew there was something strange about the relationship; however, I was given the benefit of the doubt because of my status as a leader of the ministry.

My pastor and his wife loathed to see us together (especially because I was African American from Detroit and she was Caucasian), and they made every effort to break this bond. I was threatened numerous times to end the relationship or be transferred to one of the other ministries, or released out of the ministry altogether.

I was afraid to be away from this ministry, for at this period in my life it was the only thing I knew. However, the more I valiantly tried to conclude this relationship, the more devious it became (his daughter was also warned and cautioned about her relationship with me; but she too was blinded by love and dishonesty — we both were). Eventually, she and I began sneaking around and spending time outside of the ministry's knowledge. Occasionally, I visited and picked her up from school; and at times, she came to visit me on the naval base and I took half days off from work to meet up with her at the beach or an unfamiliar location outside the normal scope of the ministry's routes/travels.

Ultimately, we discontinued meeting at undisclosed locations and began meeting at hotels, which concluded with sexual relations. In the beginning, I wept and cried because of my transgressions against God, her, and my pastor (at this summit in my life, I was saved, in love with Jesus, but deeply miserable, dejected, and confused); but then I began justifying and validating my actions and sustained this awful behavior. Jesus stated in the book of Luke 12:2:

"...everything that is covered up will be revealed, and all that is secret will be made known to everyone."

In November 1995, my ship began making its six-month deployment tour through Europe and the Mediterranean Sea. Unbeknownst to me, I received a disturbing, inconceivable, earth-shattering letter from my pastor in Norfolk – words impossible to replicate in this book. News of his daughter's relationship with me was revealed to him. As I heard the story years later, the pastor's youngest daughter along with others who knew of our relationship was finally reported and relayed to her parents. I was finally expelled (as previously warned -- receiving a lifetime ban) from the ministry and was isolated and secluded from all further communication with any person who was a current member in the ministry.

This indeed was a blessing in disguise; however, at the time, you have to understand that for the six or seven years I was in this ministry, I knew no one else or made friends with no one else (not one soul) other than those men with whom I served with in ministry. Even the brothers who were stationed on my ship with me, who came to know Jesus through my ministry, received letters from the senior pastor from Norfolk, urging them to stay away from me because I was the most wicked, immoral, corrupted, and dishonest man on the face of the earth (these words are described in modest terms).

Along with a feeling of abandonment came full-blown depression and anxiety. It was difficult for me to imagine life without this ministry. I didn't know where else I could go or what else I could do, the majority of my Christian adult life had been centered around and carved into this ministry.

Strangely, I received a letter from the bishop in Waukegan – mailed directly to my ship (he was incarcerated at the time in Illinois) – communicating his knowledge about the relationship between me and his granddaughter. His words in the letter were empathetic and apologetic, conveying his sincere prayers for me and my new journey. (I always pondered whether or not this letter was genuine or just a counterfeit strategy to keep me from revealing his dark side.)

The Christian brothers on the ship with me were in shock as to what they heard about me through written communication from the pastor. Although many of them were in disbelief as to what they read; however, they avoided me and never uttered a word to me again (thus satisfying their obligation/protocol to the leadership and the ministry). One of the more mature brothers on the ship with me (there were close to 7 of us in total) came to my sleeping quarters and made plain the information and things being said about me to damage my character. He, out of all the other men, was the only one who stood by my side (for that moment).

He stated that in his seven years of knowing me, regardless of my misfortunes, mistakes, and errors, he had not seen the things that were described about me in the letter from the pastor in Norfolk (although from that point until this day, he has never spoken to me or seen me again). For the next six months or so at sea, I was alone and traveled unaccompanied, even as we entered and exited foreign ports and destinations. Day after day, I wept bitterly, rising up nearly every day around three a.m. to pray, although I could barely move my lips to utter a sound.

I lost so much weight during that deployment that I was down to 145 lbs – practically the same weight I was when I graduated from high school. There were many sleepless and restless nights.

After my (dreadful) six-month tour at sea, my ship returned to port in Norfolk. No one on the pier greeted, celebrated, or welcomed my return home as in times past. This was one of the traditions that the ministry faithfully practiced when sailors came home from a deployment.

I was accustomed to witnessing all the "welcome home signs" with my name on them as previously displayed, but this time was different. Although I saw some familiar faces, their smiles were not to commemorate my homecoming. One of the most renowned and distinguished brothers in the ministry became the most ignored and forgotten in the blink of an eye because of the power and control of leaders in ministry and their strong influences over the minds of their members (and although I transgressed against God, there was no room for forgiveness from them toward me).

For the next year or so, I was on my own. This was the loneliest time in my entire life. My mother (with whom I was extremely close too) had recently passed away, and I was not in regular communication with my father or siblings.

Neither was I in close company with anyone else. I was completely isolated and miserable, downtrodden, and ashamed because I felt that no one would understand me. It was very unfortunate the way I departed the ministry; however, it was the key to my freedom from bondage.

I was unable to recognize the hand of Christ preparing me for a greater relationship with him. A relationship beyond meeting at a church building, beyond just words in book, but a seriousness of devotion to him molded by experience (through intense damage and anguish). Also, I was learning as they were embedded into me, the lessons of true humility, repentance, forgiveness, justification, salvation, redemption, grace, and mercy.

I cultured these attributes of Jesus Christ in a whole new light and although I became bitter with the people in that ministry for a period of time, I exchanged my bitterness toward them for forgiveness and prayed earnestly that they too would become acquainted with true meaning of salvation – recognition of the Creator in a greater measure than the created, and the power of the invisible God in greater authority than the influences of those we visibly see.

I began to observe how easy it is to set in motion a man's agenda and call it the Lord's agenda. Concurrently, Christ was tearing down the walls of deception in me: the cultish behavior and unhealthy religious traditions, my old way of thinking and living, the taught practices of Christianity (for manipulative purposes) I had been indoctrinated with – to release them and let them go.

In addition, if there was some truth to what I'd been taught – and there were a few things – Christ was refining them to me, despite the way I felt about the ministry after I was detached from it. The truth of the scriptures (after I properly studied and rightly divided them) was for me to embrace and not disregard. Presently, with the understanding of hermeneutics, hyperboles, metaphors, anthropomorphisms, apocalyptic, poetry, parables, and prophecies that comprise the Word of God, the basis of my new foundation in Christ became this passage of scripture found in the book of 1 Thessalonians 5:21:

"...but test everything that is said and hold tightly to those things that are proven to be good and wholesome...."

The dilemma with me then, and many of us today, is that we don't go back to research the scriptures for clarity in context and comprehension of the story in question. We just believe everything we hear and hold fast to things that are unproven because of the strong influence of humanity. Now out of the effects I was able to recollect, I can assure you that this information is only about 22% of religious practices that occurred through this ministry, including all the oppression and hardships suffered through this organization. It seems as though some of these events the Lord will not permit me to recall to memory; but one thing I can assure you of is that this experience was life changing.

Many brothers and sisters who were restricted to this ministry was fortunate enough not to experience the depth of soreness and adversity that I encountered; however, those who have, in like fashion, departed the ministry and regrettably a large proportion of them abandoned their passion for Christ altogether because of the corruptness of the man who portrayed a corrupted image of God. In addition, everyone who has left this ministry has been adversely affected one way or another and is in serious need of life-restoring healing (like a disease that spreads through-out the body in desperation of a cure).

I've remained in the faith – because Christ willed me to and helped me regain my confidence and spiritual conscious by rebuilding the walls of my heart to please him as I yield myself to forgiveness. I will not tell you that it was an uncomplicated and painless journey, but I will say, great is our God – my God – and greatly to be praised is His name with all acclaim and credit directed toward him. So, as I began to allow Christ to renew me, gaining some spiritual strength, I came across the path of a good friend (unassociated with the ministry), not only a good friend, but my next-door neighbor, who previously resided in the Detroit's Jeffries Housing Projects. He was also in the military and was recently transferred to Norfolk, Virginia. More importantly, he and his family had received Christ as their personal Lord and Savior, and they were a great blessing to me during my healing process period. I began spending a lot of time with him and his family, and their home became a safe haven and a place for me go after a long day of work and military duties.

As the days, months, and year progressed, I told the story of my transformation and struggles to my friend who, after my revealing the name of the church and pastor, told me that his next-door neighbor currently attended that church and that his neighbor was having a housewarming party, with their pastor as the guest speaker. Needless to say, my friend from Detroit attended the party just to meet the pastor (or should I say, interrogate the pastor), and began grilling him about me and the things that had transpired.

My friend told me that when he had approached the pastor, he was greeted with a smile, but after the conversation, the pastor was speechless and silent. Later that week, the pastor told my friend's neighbor to stay away from my friend from Detroit because, basically, he had been infected with the "Mitch Virus" (as I like to call it). Because that's how those in the ministry approached me when they saw me in public.

After my adventures with FCFC ministries and my separation from military service (after eight and a half years), I remained in the Virginia area for an additional nine years before making my way back to the Motor City. In those additional nine years in Virginia, I never made contact with the pastor from FCFC, although I wanted to for the sake of peace and restoration. I was told he was still bitter toward me and had not forgiven me, but remained fervent to harm me. (In recent months, the pastor's daughter and I, miraculously, made contact with each other through Facebook; for peace, clarity, forgiveness and healing purposes).

So, as the world turned and me with it, I gradually grew in confidence and in the grace of

God, and I progressively healed from being disgraced, destitute, and literally left for dead (both physically and spiritually). One summer afternoon, I met up with my neighbor from Detroit for a game of billiards on one of the naval bases in Norfolk. As we were playing, he introduced me to one his friends who I bumped into again on one of the military base basketball courts. Later, the friend of my friend repeatedly asked me to visit his church; and, as I had promised him, I kept my word and attended his house of worship.

Then, over the next six months after visiting his church, I became a member of the ministry (BTC). Here I went once more, making an effort to become part of what I believed to be a whole new and different expedition and experience (learning how to trust all over again). My first involvement in Christian ministry was with a Caucasian pastor and a diverse congregation (with the majority of the leadership being Caucasian). But this new ministry was more of an African American persuasion with the majority of black leaders. Still recovering from being broken and banged-up spiritually, I committed myself to this new ministry, however, this time -- with a little more knowledge and wisdom due to my previous experiences.

This is the story of my second ministry at BTC – an eight-year outing. Between the transformations from FCFC ministries to BTC, I was not a member of an organization in any Christian ministry; however, I was intertwined with Christ every day. For many religious people that is somewhat hard to fathom, because almost everyone has been taught to equate and limit Christ to an organization/building with flawless attendance (as if Christ only dwells in buildings on Sunday mornings). Although I knew and clearly understood that I would have to learn how to trust people again, my mindset going into this next ministry was discovering and identifying the basis and root of my previous pains and struggles so that I would not repeat these similar occurrences, nor be repetitively entangled in bondage. The calamities that transpired in my life were an unparalleled lesson in promoting my future.

Now, the history with my second ministry started out pleasant and sturdy; and before I knew it, I was again quickly promoted in the ministry and assigned to assist my new bishop in pastoral functions. For those who are not familiar with the duties of pastoral ministry, it is someone the ministry considers dependable and readily available to support the necessities of the pastoral staff, including guest leaders, aiding both special and confidential requirements. Although I was newly married in this season of my life, I traveled with the bishop and leadership team on a regular basis across this immense country, probably more than his own wife and elders.

There was a small group of men, along with me, who were appointed and tasked to serve the bishop (at home and abroad). Because of our willingness to serve God and man, many of us were speedily elevated in ministry. However, because of my previous experiences, I wasn't so enthusiastic about bearing more responsibilities, for I clearly understood this unspoken spiritual practice for leaders – meaning:

> *"the more you witnessed events – the more you became blinded," and "the more you carried others' burdens – the heavier you became."*

The vagueness behind this allegory is simple: as a leader you are required to survey obsessions that are beyond belief – distant from biblical principles – then it becomes essential for you as a leader to become insensitive, thoughtless, and deadened to the activities you've just witnessed. Furthermore, the moment you became responsive to these uncharacteristic behaviors, the heavier you became physically, spiritually, and emotionally – that is, if you haven't already become numb to reality.

I'm not speaking about judging another man's or woman's shortcomings, for we all have sinned and repeatedly fall short of the glory of God. Neither am I suggesting perfection in the midst of human error; but there should be a sense of maturity and progression in faith and in life. But, more importantly, what I'm concerned with is the repetitive practices of immorality committed without empathy, remorse, and repentance by those who are expected to know better through salvation.

Some leaders think it is their right to function in a manner that's unbiblical and unethical because of their position, title, or status of authority in ministry, as if once they reach a certain position in Christianity or any other religion, they are exempt from the standards set by Christ and His Word. Although contrary to popular belief, serving God is not the same as serving man. In fact, we should never serve (as to becoming a slave to) a man, woman, organization, or anything that limits our commitment to Christ.

No bonus points are rewarded for serving in ministry if we are not committed to serving God in fellowship by prayer, by love, with joy and tranquility, which requires faith that's expanded by hearing the Word of God as we study and rightly divide it (by not adding our own thoughts and meanings to it, but observing the context of what's already written), as we become more and more acquainted with performing it (living as born-again believers according to the Word of

God). Although we are required to unify in the body of Christ and serve one another, there are no biblical implications that state we must serve mankind or an entity (His creation) like we are expected to serve God (The Creator); neither are there biblical references that denotes if you became the servant to the flesh of another human being that God is well pleased with you. But, as the Bible clearly and distinctly states, "Love your neighbor (fellow citizen) as you would love yourself," and "Treat your neighbor as you would want to be treated."

We are not biblically required to love or serve our neighbors in the same approach in which we are constrained to love and serve God, because God is superior to man in every sense of the word "superior." Our love and service toward God should be demonstrated in a way that transcends our love and servitude toward one another. In fact, we learn how to love and serve each other by our personal commitment and love we demonstrate toward God, which is loving him enough to keep and practice His way of living.

To simplify, we are not expected to worship humanity (in a sense of total devotion), and praise humanity (in a sense of highly exulting), or idolize humanity (in a sense of a statue or deity of worship), including those we adore and honor.

For we are made in the image and likeness of God, and because God is a Spirit, the image and likeness we share with Him is being made with the "Spirit of life," which encompasses the soul of mankind (our conscience – which intertwines our sense of right and wrong, our will, our mind, our intellect and emotions). Then the creation (our living spirit and conscience) in which God personally handcrafted, designed, and given His seal of approval: He infused in human flesh - formed and made from the dust of the earth.

After serving for a period of time at BTC, I was approached by the bishop to consider working full time (paid staff) as the administrative assistant of the church, adding that he believed this was the will of God for me to act upon. So, after a short time in prayer, I resolved in my own mind that this recommendation was God's plan for my life.

See, the Word of the Lord encourages us in the book of Romans 12:2 not to be conformed (meaning being fashioned, tailored, and custom-made) to this world, this generation, this age, but be transformed (changed) by renewing our minds (renewing our thought patterns from our past behaviors) with new ideas and attitudes generated by God, so we may PROVE for ourselves HIS good will for us, HIS acceptable will for us, which will ultimately translate us toward HIS perfect (mature/complete) will for us.

So, whenever someone tells you what they believe to be God's will for you/me, we must recognize that God's will is not for anyone else to determine or interpret. You (the individual) must establish His will through prayer and supplication, through experiment and miscalculations, through testing and time. No one has the right to determine God's will for you – except you and God alone. People can suggest and guesstimate, but it is your decisive responsibility to discover and distinguish His will for your life (in every phase of your existence) according to HIS already spoken and written word.

So, in your life's journey toward understanding God's definitive will for YOU, in the event you fall short of HIS will (which both you and I will do), we can take courage and rest in the fact that our shortcomings were derived from our own choices rather than the preferences and selections generated by others and their private agendas. In January 2001, I resigned from my place of employment at Verizon (in sales, making about $35,000 a year) and chose to work full time for the ministry (with a salary of $29,000 a year, with a wife and two children to support).

The first couple of months in the ministry as a full-time employee went well. Then, in the third month, something interesting happened. The bishop called me into his office for a two-month review to evaluate my performance, then inquired about my opinion of the position. He had spent most of his dialogue comparing me to the previous employee (who no longer worked there and was quietly terminated), hoping I would implement some of those previous practices.

I've heard various people make this remark, *"If it's not broke, don't fix it."* But I always deliberated in this manner: *"Although it's not broke, find ways for perpetual improvements."* Why hire a new employee with innovative ideas to come and maintain the old way of doing business with no space for change, growth, and enhancement? Where would this world be today, where would you and I be today, without movements and progress, modifications and adjustments, development and technology?

So, after the Bishop gave me his thoughts on my performance, he asked me a question and stated: *"Son, if there's anything I can do to make your job better, feel free at any time to inform me or my wife (who was the acting administrator) so we can make accommodations to support your ability to perform."*

Then I stated, *"Yes! There is something you can do to make my routine better."* Then I explained to him that when he gives me tasks to accomplish (in an eight-hour workday – it can be anywhere from 15 to 20 different lengthy assignments), could he inform me about the precedence of each task so I can prioritize the workload and complete the most important assignments first.

Suddenly, his whole countenance altered and he looked really annoyed. The he stated: *"Are you accusing me and my wife of being out of order?"* (In church talk that means being double-minded or being inconsistent.) He took my request to mean that he (as a pastor) didn't know what he was doing or what he was doing wasn't good enough and required urgent revisions; although his methods were indeed antiquated and called for expansion, my motives were wholesome. Furthermore, in my courting stages, prior to employment there, he informed me that one of the reasons he desired to hire me was to improve the functioning and operations of the church's office.

In amazement, I responded, *"No, sir, Pastor. That was not my objective."* Then I elaborated that I was just responding to his offer, "If there's anything I can do to make your job better...".

However, they (my pastor and his wife) received and held my comment as a hostile approach. This was the beginning of more dark and gloomy days as the ministry's new employee and member of the church. (I was a member of the church for four years prior to becoming a full-time employee.)

Again, at this stage in my life I'd recently married my childhood friend, Bridget (who came to visit me in my previous ministry), whom I'd known well over 20 years prior to marriage. She and I, along with her sister and brother, and my sisters, were all friends and grew up together. After having absolutely no communication with her approximately three years aforementioned, we became reacquainted as friends (at that time in my life when I really needed a friend) and later married. Year after year, I learned more and more about my bishop, as I'm sure he did about me. To continue my downward spiral as an employee and member of the church, my bishop began telling me that I ponder too much and that I should do less thinking and more following of his every command, as this was how I would learn obedience.

There had been times when my opinions were solicited and I did not agree with him, so he began labeling me as someone who thinks/analyzes too much, or someone who is contentious and dangerous.

Many leaders follow that same trend of thinking. The notion that if someone disagrees with them, then they are disagreeing with God, as if God himself is required to obey and agree with their behavior, thought patterns, and the directions of every leader. The bishop blatantly ignored all the new changes that were implemented in the office shortly after he had given his consent for me to revise office policies and procedures for future employees, and best practices for improving workload management. Instead, he increased the workload and expected it all to be completed by the end of the workday. This ministry was the "mother church" and headquarters to seven other churches affiliated with BTC, recognized and known as the

"Gethsemane Family of Churches." So my job intensified because I was solely responsible for handling the business and social aspects among all eight ministries.

I was doing the work of four administrators but getting paid less than one, based on the conversations I had with other church administrators in the area. (And again, I was merely the administrative assistant. The bishop's wife was the administrator whose sole responsibility was to issue paychecks for all the employees, which consisted of her husband, herself, me, and the custodian.) When I was unable to finish one of the many assignments given to me by the bishop, he strongly accused me of having a dreadful mind and stated that I was too absentminded, with an inclination to disregard.

He even asked me if, when I was a teenager, did I smoked a lot of marijuana or used drugs, because he believed there was something wrong with my thinking process and my ability to retain information. While he was out of town, he frequently called the church office just to find error and uncover mistakes associated with the way I conducted the churches' business. I mean, he literally screamed at me over the phone to remind me how forgetful I was and tried to convince me that his ideas were better and that he was much smarter because he was the bishop.

I was baffled and perplexed because I was not in competition with him (as I often stated) because I was content with being me, though there was a period I doubted and questioned myself because of him. The relationship between us became so strained that it was physically and mentally painful and tiresome for me to even to go to work each morning because I knew I would be accused of something. The immense problem all along was that I was not a person who agreed with everyone's agenda just because of a title, but I did my very best to align my views with the word of God and the person in question to include myself. At that moment in time, I only confided in my wife and the Lord and did not share my personal business with my bishop or anyone who couldn't see beyond the bishop and his dreams. One time, when my wife and I were standing in the church's hallway as the bishop was passing by, he gingerly greeted my wife, asked her how she was doing, then uttered in a comical way that her husband keeps to himself with little to no confiding in him. Eventually, I pursued a college education, and when I graduated with my associate degree in science, the bishop was infuriated because I hadn't solicited his counsel nor sought his approval. When I furthered my education even more and obtained my bachelor's degree in business management, he literally ignored me and my accomplishments.

For a period of time, he walked past my office and did not voice a word (in salutation) to me. On one particular Sunday morning, he was acknowledging the members' accomplishments and achievements, noting that the church would distribute $25 dollars for members who recently graduated with their high school diploma, $30 dollars for members who recently graduated from a trade school of some sort, $50 dollars for those who graduated with their associate degrees, and $100 dollars for all other higher degrees. The bishop's wife (the current administrator) was tasked with getting the names of all the members who had recently graduated. During that Sunday morning service, the bishop graciously read all the names and passed out the gifts for those who recently graduated – and my name was tactfully omitted. When my name was not announced, my wife raised her hand and affirmed that her husband had recently graduated with his bachelor's degree (keep in mind that I was an employee and part of the church's staff).

Another staff member (the custodian) graduated with a certificate in heating/cooling and he was not overlooked. After my wife acknowledged my accomplishments, they acted as if it was an oversight on their behalf and in about a week I received something. I told my wife that if she had not raised her hand on my behalf, I wouldn't have thought twice about it (meaning whether or not I received any special recognition from them was unimportant to me at the time).

Although I believe this particular bishop was a good man, with first-class intentions in his commencement of the ministry, his vulnerable spot, which hindered the progress and growth of the ministry, was his insecurity about himself and his latest quest in obtaining the almighty dollar. When someone joined the ministry and demonstrated gifts and talents the bishop did not possess, if he could not control that person/individual, his insecurities pressured those members to either conform to his standards or leave the ministry.

More often than not, the members usually obeyed his call. There will be many who may ask, "Why were you a member of this second ministry for such a long time, especially after experiencing the unwarranted hardship from my first ministry?" My reply would be similar to the responses of many others: I felt obligated and stuck with my commitment to the ministry, and I didn't know who else I could turn to or where else to go. And, although I was married, I did not want to approach that same state of loneliness as in times past. The one thing this bishop had going for him was his ability to mesmerize his followers through the gift of the prophetic – the ability to prophesy (whether these sayings came to pass or not). I soon learned that people earnestly yearn for spiritual gifts in a greater measure than those who sincerely desire the Giver of those gifts, and will chase after the working of signs and wonders more than the one who is the Wonderful Sign.

On a weekly basis, for about eight years, we went to Sunday school beginning at 10 a.m. The Sunday morning services began around 11 a.m. and concluded sometime between 3 p.m. and 5 p.m. After praise and worship and collecting money, he preached the whole Bible, from Genesis to Revelations, and ended every service by prophesying and praying for the whole church, including all visitors, praying for each person on a individual basis, speaking things that fed people's appetites (gave them what they wanted to hear), and many flocked to him. Ironically, whenever he prayed for me – laying his hands on my forehead – he never expressed a word except to note that God was going to bless me, then he nudged me to go and be seated (that was usually the extent and routine prayer from him to me).

His teaching and preaching abilities were average (not based on style, but in the ability to convey the simplicity of the gospel); however, he was sure to give you a private word of prophecy every Sunday afternoon. (If you were in leadership, you were required to remain in attendance until he had completed his prophesying. Then and only then were you released to go home and spend the little time you had left in that day to enjoy with your own family.)

Furthermore, if you were in leadership and wanted to depart the service prior to his prayer of approval, he attempted to humiliate you and make you feel guilty by making statements such as, *"If you have to go, then leave, but you might miss your blessings,"* or *"If you have to depart, then exit, but Jesus is still here."*

What appeared to be excellent and well built in the beginning became appalling and feeble at the height of its continuation. My channel of communication is from experience, not unproven information or unconfirmed reports. I was engaged in many pastors-only and staff meetings, conversations, arguments, and so forth and so on. The average church attendee may never have the opportunity to observe the things I saw, or take notice of the things I heard in the duration of their Christianity, not the average Christian (and this is not something I'm boasting about or take pride in, but I'm just stating a noticeable reality).

My dialogue extends beyond the perspective of my bishop or previous ministry; but, because of my contact and visitation with various leaders in several states, I'm saying you wouldn't believe some of the things that take place in the name of the Lord. Now I have personally witnessed and worked with some great men and women of God who walked with great integrity (regardless of private mistakes), but these types of leaders and ministries, more often than not, go unnoticed, disregarded, and are a rare group in the era of Christianity (because many are searching for ministries with the "fireworks" appearance of popularity: explosive and eye-catching in outward show, without deploying proper love and nurture for the people of God). In addition, I witnessed the integrity of my bishop diminish as he became less of a leader to God's people and more of a servant to those dead presidents or founding fathers printed on green paper: wishing himself to be treated like royalty on every occasion.

This was partly due to the number of leaders we both came in contact with as we traveled abroad. Most of his good friends who served on the same level of leadership possessed more wealth than he, while simultaneously prompting him of his worthiness to more luxury. Soon after, due to his ability to prophesy, he felt he deserved to have the best of everything and added that it was God's will for his life. (Sound familiar?) From January 2001 to December 2005, this ministry averaged around 300 members, of which 150 of these members were children under the age of

18, with no occupation. With nearly 150 adults, this ministry grossed virtually a half million dollars annually. In a very active year, there were more than 30 guest speakers who visited the church, preached a sermon, and were compensated; some with hotel accommodations, meals, and incidentals paid for by the ministry. All the church's bills, loans, utilities, etc., were an estimated $90,000 dollars for that particular year (that was the highest I had observed in an average year in this ministry). At the time, my salary was $29,000, the custodian's salary (with a wife and five children) was around $24,000, and the bishop kept at least $50,000-$60,000 spare in the church's general account. (i.e., when you subtract the expenses from the average annual gross income; the remainder after the expenses was in the area of $357,000 net).

My purpose in enlightening you about the ministry's funding is in no way negative criticism; it's more a way of educating many of you in the realization of where/how your money is used and delegated. Although I have had many of my companions argue that when they give, they bestow unto the Lord and are not concerned about how their money is expended or exhausted. My dispute in defense always was:

"Just how do you really give unto the Lord when he owns everything? When we donate our finances, we are giving to an institution we deem to be honorable and trustworthy, as it is our responsibility as stakeholders in the ministry to be aware and knowledgeable about the path of our investments." (And, in this regard, scores of people are oblivious and naïve.)

Then I usually end with a statement such as, "How many of you place your money in the stock market without being concerned about it collapsing and you losing your life's savings?" (As was realistically demonstrated with so many of us within the past decade or so.) And, "Why then would you invest in a ministry in this same fashion (such as the stock market) without any care or concern about its expansion or depletion?"

Again, I am not implying that you stay away from giving to the ministry of Christianity (because it is vital and essential to further the good news of Christ), but I am implying that it's time for you to give more consideration and attention to your resources as you already do in the other areas of your life – giving it the same reverence and significance as you would with everything else regarding your money. So, with only 150 employed adults in the ministry, the bishop's salary initially was $100,000 annually, and I remember him directing one of the elders who were a high-ranking member on the church's board to initiate legislature that would increase his wages. Independent from his annual salary, the ministry funded his monthly mortgage payments on his home, his and his wife's automobiles, their automobile fuel expenses, their clothing expenses, and 25% of the church's income, not expunged from his annual salary, was applied to his/her life insurance policies and mutual funds accounts.

Because I was one of the bishop's personal armor bearers (as described in biblical terms, but only meaning his private "caretaker"), as well as the church's administrative assistant, I paid the church's utility bills, credit card bills, and handled the majority of the expenses in general. And so I was privileged and exposed to an assortment of information. With all of these funds going in his favor, people were still strongly inspired and encouraged (commonly by the leadership and other guest ministers/pastors) to give more money in support of the bishop, his wife, and two younger children: for their birthday celebrations, their wedding anniversary, the ministry's anniversary, his pastoral anniversary, and Pastors' Appreciation Month for the entire month of August each year.

The most common quotation used to defuse his gain of wealth (as do many) was, "You can't beat God giving," as a subliminal message to convey to God's people that "The more you supply for me and my cause – the more God will provide toward you and your wishes." Furthermore, what he gained through only 150 adults was an annual base salary of $100,000, without having to use any of it toward any of his personal expenses, and yearly royalties achieved through the ministry – and it wasn't enough. He required more wealth. His immoral financial appetite became more evident from year to year. The more the ministry increased statistically and economically, the more his earnings grew without focusing primarily on the ministry's needs, as well as the necessities of others, especially those who were loyal members and faithfully gave to the ministry.

Although this type of behavior is common in many ministries, it is not warranted/suitable for leaders to conduct themselves biblically in this fashion. The Apostle Paul warns Timothy about these type of money gluttony and self-indulgent customs as noted in the book of 1 Timothy 6:9-10, describing leaders who are tarnished in mind and misled of the truth, who imagine that gain is godliness, or righteousness as a source of profit, a moneymaking business as a means of livelihood for themselves. But this type of behavior is selfish and uncharitable to the poor, especially toward those who are less fortunate and are an everyday support to the ministry.

It is also inconsiderate and uncaring of those who are struggling monetarily, but continuously aid in support of the ministry and its requests. Although the ministry has its needs, it is not the same as the leader's pursuit for personal greed, and I am not advocating that leaders should remain poor; but I am promoting that leaders should not take an unfair/unreasonable advantage of their vocation in Christ – confusing their calling from God with being hired as a Chief Executive Officer (CEO)/Chief Financial Officer (CFO) as in a corporation or business.

Now I'm fully conscious of how many will stand in defense/protection of their leaders and ministry, emphatically stating that their organization does not behave in such a manner. However, I would like to call your attention to a passage of scripture in the book of 2 Corinthians 2:17. The Apostle Paul states: *"For we are not like so many, (like hucksters making a trade of) peddling God's Word (shortchanging and adulterating the divine message)...."*

This opening of scripture does not propose that every leader and ministry under Heaven is dishonest and not striving to live a respectable and productive life, but Paul, in fact, stated these three words, *"like so many."* In addition, it is time that we (the body of Christ) cease from manufacturing programs, workshops, and extra curriculum praise services just for the sake of collecting money.

People are being financially drained without any remorse from spiritual leaders; proclaiming that if you give more – God will give you more; but yet, those are not the equivalent standards from which they live. I have been in attendance as a witness in various pastor/leadership seminars where the primary agenda was consistently on the subject of money and how to get the people of God to give more money without them feeling like it's a burden; this is often accomplished by using biblical principles out of context without applying the proper meaning. The goal to completing this task was usually when the leadership creates this incredible vision of God raining treasures from heaven with the promises of material blessings.

If God's chief focus was to fulfill our lives with earthly treasures or the abundance of wealth – as so often proclaimed; why do we still have so many poor citizens living in this world; moreover, why do we still have so many Christians in our ministry who are struggling financially and who are living below the poverty level – RIGHT IN OUR CHURCHES! Did not Christ state that the life is more (greater in quality) than meat/food and the body is more (above and beyond) than raiment or clothing? In other words, God value our lives far greater than our capacity to achieve wealth.

I was one of those members, as it is biblically stated, "who would run through a troop and leap over a wall" for my leaders, to illustrate/pledge my loyalty to them; but now I truly comprehend, after so many years, that my devotion, my allegiance, my faithfulness, and my lifestyle must first be established with God and him alone; then from my servitude toward God, these qualities and characteristics will be shown and known in the midst of all people. God is the only being who can keep his promise when he stated that "he'll never leave us nor forsake us."

This is one of the main reasons why countless souls are bitter with God and Christianity today because many have cast their lives at the mercy and feet of their leaders in hopes that their leaders would never leave, forsake, mislead, or disappoint them. Furthermore, when the foundation of their hopes/expectations from humanity begins to crumble, many find themselves angry with God and blame him for their tragedies. But Christianity 101 tells us in the book of Proverbs 3:5-7:

"Lean on, trust in, and be confident in the Lord with all of your heart and do not rely on your own insight or understanding. In all your ways know, recognize, and acknowledge Him and he will direct and make straight your paths...."

In my opinion, the biggest error in the realm of Christianity is that we don't read/interpret the Bible in context (with the use of other biblical references) for ourselves. We give consent and freedom to everyone/everything else around us to construe our lives rather than submit our will to the Creator of it.

After traveling with my bishop, and upon his return, I remember he waited until Sunday morning (during service) to advise the members that the other ministries he visited treated him better than his own church family. He told the church that when David made the statement in the book of Psalms: "Lift up ye heads all ye gates and be lifted up ye everlasting doors and the king of glory shall come in." that the word "heads" interpreted in that passage of scripture meant we should lift him up. The sad thing is, many members did so accordingly, although "heads," as described in the book of Psalms, were wooden circular pillars that stood at each end of massive gates. Affixed to these wooden circular pillars were rings of iron with chains nestled within them.

When the ark of the covenant (representing God's presence) approached the entrance of David's Kingdom, these chains, which were fastened to the iron rings connected to the wooden heads located on each end of these enormous gates, King David prompted the lifting up of these heads in lieu of the gates, allowing the presence of God/the ark of the covenant to freely enter into his courts.

Also, I began hearing the Bishop utter things like "God will not speak to us if we didn't learn to obey his voice as well as the voice of his wife"; and that "God personally told him that his members do not have a connection with Him (God) because many of his members don't have a close relationship with him (the Bishop) as their Father". Furthermore, he implored us that if anyone did not comprehend the things that he and his wife were saying; through obedience to him, we were still required to walk in submission to him without understanding, because we should trust that he is God's mouthpiece.

And the sad thing is, this is the identical posture which he lives by today as many continue to trail the tone of his voice. While I was employed in this ministry, I confidentially began keeping a diary and recording everything that took place, just to assuage some type of insanity within myself – for this burden I was digesting momentarily was too great to share with anyone (for no one under his influence would receive it anyway); and the little I shared with my wife on occasion was heartbreaking for her to even hear.

I began writing this diary mainly due to the amount of verbal abuse I was receiving and enduring. Years later, I revealed this diary to a friend (a mature leader of high esteem) who was speechless and could not even fathom the things he read, especially about this bishop and ministry. To him it became believable because he was an eyewitness of the consistency of my temperament (not claiming perfection) and an immediate spectator to the loyalty shown from me toward this bishop and ministry (for numerous years) by the grace of God.

I continued with this ministry for eight consecutive years because I feared awful things would happen to my family without the bishop's permission to depart the ministry. He instilled in us a belief that getting his permission was getting God's permission. During this eight-year period, this bishop attempted to strip me of my mind, my wisdom and knowledge, my dignity, my character, and my calling because I declined to be in 100% agreement with him as he thought I should have been because I was one of his privileged staff members.

In December 2005, I finally began trusting that Christ is bigger than this ministry or any ministry. I sat down with my bishop, face to face, and told him that I was parting ways with him and the ministry, as my time with them had expired. He became even more bitter with me. During our conversation, I had to progressively stop him from angrily yelling and lashing out and force him to take a few minutes to just hear my thoughts from the depths of my heart.

As he silently listened, I perceived by his facial expression that he showed no interest in what I desired for my own life, nor did he show any interest toward my wife and family. Until then, every ounce of my being had been poured as cement into building monuments to him, his family, and the ministry; and, in a blink of an eye, it all became ancient history and went unnoticed. Every member who decided to move on was treated in this same manner.

Yes, I love God and, yes, I am a servant of God, but in all honesty, at that time, I also prized and served this bishop concurrently with serving the

Lord, although you and I both know, that you cannot serve two masters (persons, places, or things and God). Eventually, for the sake of his own embarrassment and for the sake of him maintaining his own ego and followers, he began spreading false rumors as to why my family and the others departed the ministry, as relayed by a pastor/friend of mine who was shocked at the news. He also labeled us as cancerous and rebels, threatening those who remained that if they decided to leave, their fate would be just as bitter as those who had departed the ministry.

Today, I couldn't be more blessed and at peace; and to this day, I am not bitter with him or the ministry – this includes the prior ministry because I refuse to live a life of resentment and animosity. Through time, I healed. I've forgiven and I've moved on and now moving forward; however, I will not be silent but will provide support to those who desire it and require it. And this next phase of my life, the life of my family, our purpose and employment to include the current ministry that I share in association and communion with God, will be gratifying because of the knowledge and wisdom gained from life's dreadful experiences. I will not allow myself or my family to be bound and governed by church religious policies and procedures that negatively impact my/our life. Christ died for me so that I can freely serve him and that I endeavor to accomplish.

As the word of God so eloquently states in 2 Corinthians 4:17:

"For our present troubles are small and will not last very long. Yet they continue to produce for us an exceptionally and endless weight of glory that vastly outweighs our troubles. So, we don't repeatedly gaze at the present dilemmas visibly seen; but rather, we fix our eyes on things that cannot be noticeably observed. For the things we distinguish now are temporary and will not last forever, but the things we cannot see are perpetual and endless."

My exposure to Christian conduct (in the areas of pastoral and leadership) was ordained and purposed for me, even though at the time it was not a good position in which to be placed. I've gained a wealth of awareness and information regarding the diversity of organizations that I developed through my travels in both ministries and my exposure to various ethnicities.

In June 2006, I spent my last days in Virginia, and returned to Michigan where I've spiritually grown in leaps and bounds, living better physically, spiritually, emotionally, and mentally. In addition, when I returned to Michigan, I destroyed my diary as a sign of a new beginning, although I should have kept it as a reminder of where I had been and where God has brought me from – and my continual appreciation for his grace and mercy on my life and for giving me salvation through the message of Jesus Christ.

This is my testimony and story, and I know many of you have much to share as well. Despite all you have gone through, don't give up on God or divorce Christ or Christianity and its ideology. Please know that God is not holding you hostage in a ministry where Christ is not the single center of attention. If you are in a situation where you're spiritually anemic, you may choose to depart and seek God in a place with greener pastures and living waters, so He can restore your soul and lead you down the path of righteousness for His name's sake.

Some may state that there is no such thing as a "perfect church," and in some regards that statement holds value; however, there is such a thing called "a mature church," where God's people function in honesty, humility, and true love; where Christ is the hero and man is the zero; and God's people are not held in control and bondage. You may not find a ministry on this planet without errors but you can find ministries that are mature. Jesus tells us in the book of St. Matthew 7:7-8:

"Keep on asking, and you'll continuously receive what you're asking for. Keep on seeking, and you will continuously find what you're looking for. Keep on knocking, and the door will continuously open for you."

Being consistent with persistence brings about gradual change, but being continuously stagnant keeps you permanently confined.

CHAPTER *3*

BEWARE OF FALSE PROPHETS

The Bible clearly warns us to "beware" of false prophets. Did you know that the subject matter regarding false prophets is a major focal point of discussion found in biblical literature (subsequent to topics such as love, redemption, and salvation)? However, it's also one of the least conversed about, overlooked topics among the body of believers. Just think about this: When was the last time you heard a lecture or teaching in your church, synagogue, or cathedral on the subject matter? More importantly, when was the last time you/I picked up the Bible to research and explore this area of dialogue? Does it even come to mind? My personal opinion on this question is simply this: Many of those who fall into the category of false prophets may be those we greatly admire and highly esteem; and there's no way this person, the one I allow to have the most influence in my/our lives (outside of God himself) can be a false prophet, teacher, or minister. So, who are the false prophets and how are they identified? Are they tall or short; black or white; long-haired or bald? Are they usually irate or pleasant; do they smile or frown; are they strangers or someone I recognize. Do they identify themselves by wearing a T-shirt that has the word "false" on the front side and the word "prophet" written on the back?

Sounds humorous, but many people look for the physical signs of an individual to determine deceit; however, the Bible clearly outlines the characteristics of false prophets based on pretense and fabrication. Before we get into the particulars, let's biblically define these two words: both the Hebrew and Greek definition for word "false" (or pseudo) means one who intentionally lies, demonstrates deceit, expresses dishonesty, knowingly fraudulent, consciously deceptive, and deliberately counterfeit.

The word "prophet" which encompasses the words "prophecy or prophesy" means one who proclaims or speaks forth (i.e., to announce, notify, to inform) and foretells (the forecasting of future events). Although there are distinct differences between the office of a prophet and one who is divinely inspired to speak, the rules of engagement apply in both cases. Whenever a message is declared on behalf of God, this message must be completely in conformity with God's divine will and purpose in correlation to His already spoken word. Case in point!

John the Baptist was characterized by Jesus Christ as being one of the greatest prophets ever born of a woman; however, John the Baptist's ministry was to prepare the way of the Lord by preaching the message of repentance, not foretelling futures. He never predicted his audiences' futures, never told them they were getting new donkeys, new houses, more money, or even finding soul mates. John the Baptist was a prophet who announced the doctrine of repentance and influenced people to confess their sins. Jesus also asserted the message of repentance to include salvation (deliverance) with the ability to forgive sin. Based on biblical history, no records illustrate that John the Baptist preached about himself, proclaiming the message of salvation for money, fame, fortune, prestige, or gaining material wealth. The true message that comes from God is not self-focused but always about the glorification of God and His will, a hundred percent of the time.

In the book of Romans 12: 1-2, the Apostle Paul implores the body of believers by saying:

"And so, dear brothers and sisters, I plead with you to give your bodies to God because of all he has done for you. Let them be a living and holy sacrifice – the kind he will find acceptable. This is truly the way to worship him. Don't copy the behavior and customs of this world, but let God transform you into a new person by changing the way you think. Then you will learn to know God's will for you, which is good and pleasing and perfect."

How interesting is that; we'll learn God's will for our life when we do not imitate the manners and morals dictated by society, influencing us to live based on the current standards of life. Understanding God's will begins when we allow him to change who we are by changing the way we think; and that, my friends, does not come by seeking someone to stimulate us with words that appeal to our sensual nature, through prophesy.

Furthermore, we will discover that many prophets (both Old and New Testament) rarely prophesied about gaining wealth and being rich, neither fame nor fortune. Biblically, false prophets were identified as those who misleadingly proclaimed messages divinely inspired by God, although some possessed the distinct ability to foretell future events and manufacture miracles, signs, and wonders. According to biblical writings, false prophets fell into three general categories:

- Those who worshiped false gods and served idols;
- Those who falsely claimed to receive messages from the Lord;

- Those who wandered from the truth and ceased to be true prophets.

The last category is by far the most dangerous of the three, *"Those who wandered from the truth and ceased to be true prophets,"* because many people cannot identify when their favorite influential leader has turned away from living and speaking truth, and has begun articulating myths/falsehoods to achieve recognition, prosperity, and influence (which equates to self-indulgence in favor of material wealth/greed, lust for money/sex, and dominance over God's people), while at the same time becoming insensitive to God's will and the spiritual needs of His children.

Many ministries and organizations resemble businesses and corporations for profit only and border on entertainment (with music awards/idol stars) rather than the place to honor and worship the most High God with the attention solely directed toward him. In the Old Testament, Balaam was a prophet who had an affiliation with God and heard from God. There was a Moabite leader by the name of Balak who despised the nation of Israel and desired to conquer them severely, but he understood that His armies were defenseless against the Hebrew nation because of God's favor and protection on His people. Balak recognized that he could not defeat God's people with external forces; however, he had a clear awareness of Israel's history with idolatry and their ability (as a nation) to defeat themselves from within by idol worship or practices. Balak searched for someone able to infiltrate the nation of Israel from within. When Balak heard about Balaam the prophet, he sent his men to retrieve him. When the men were face to face, Balak pleaded with Balaam (a recognizable prophet) and urged him to curse God's people from within.

God himself gave Balaam a message and told him to speak only those words that he (God) had given him to verbalize to Balak. After sacrificing on seven altars and hearing from God, the prophet Balaam went to Balak and blessed God's people instead of cursing them. Balaam even made this profound statement to Balak regarding

God's people, found in the book of Numbers 22:18:

"Even if Balak were to give me his palace filled with silver and gold, I would be powerless to do anything against the will of the Lord my God."

The writings established in the Old Testament with reference to Balaam and Balak concludes with Balaam blessing God's people, then returning home. If Balaam was not a prophet of God (in the infancy stages of his life), or if Balaam was a wicked prophet never having any relationship with God (as many allude to), how could he have the power to bless God's people; why would God use him to carry the word of truth to another person on his behalf, and why would the scriptures reference Balaam as a man who hears directly from God? (Numbers Chapters 22-25)

But the story doesn't end there. The New Testament epistles mention Balaam in several passages: Peter speaks of false teachers who *"have forsaken the right way and gone astray, following the way of Balaam."* (2 Peter 2:15)

Jude speaks of backsliders who *"have run greedily in the error of Balaam for profit."* (Jude 1:11)

Yes, even Balaam, the one who once blessed God's people turned away from dealing truthfully and began taking bribes. Balaam's error was greed and covetousness and he was paid well to cause Israel to curse themselves from within the nation/within the body of God. The nature of Balaam's curse is made clear by John in the book of Revelations. It refers to some members of the church in Pergamos who held *"the doctrine of Balaam,"* who taught Balak to put a stumbling block before the children of Israel, to eat things sacrificed to idols, and to commit sexual immorality (in which they were forbidden to partake of and practice (Revelation 2:14).

Prior to Balaam departing from Balak (the Moabite leader), there is apparent evidence that Balaam the prophet educated Balak about Israel's history of idolatry; and that Israel could be defeated from within if they were seduced to worship and follow Baal (the idol god), to eat things sacrificed to idols, and to practice sexual immorality. The Bible clearly demonstrates this act of abandonment and shows us exactly what happens to the nation of Israel immediately after the departure of Balaam: The children of Israel began to commit harlotry with the women of Moab. The practice of prostitution between the men of Israel and the women of Moab united the two nations. In celebration, the nation of Israel was invited by the Moabites to the sacrifices of their gods, and the Moabite people ate and bowed down to their gods.

Because of their affiliation with this nation, the scriptures enlighten us that Israel was eventually joined to the idol god Baal of Peor and the wrath of the Lord was provoked and in opposition to Israel (Numbers 25:1-3). Many scholars argue Balaam's relationship with God, but the passages of scripture clearly identify a positive and constructive relationship between God and Balaam. Balaam, a prophet of God who started on the right path, ended in destruction and led a whole nation of people into devastation.

This is what happens when true leaders turn sour and continue leading God's people into oblivion (while pretending to practice Christianity in a denominational or nondenominational setting). This practice of deception is ultimately noticed in their extracurricular standard of living, which is grounded and rooted in materialism devoted to self-pleasure. In condemning the "way of the Balaam," the New Testament expresses disapproval of those who are led astray by greed while simultaneously enticing God's people to compromise their moral principles and values.

In the Old Testament, Moses spoke of the chastisement for those who became disloyal to the faith, and gave approval to stone any prophet who advocated the worship of other gods (Deuteronomy 13:1-18). During the period of power and reign of King Ahab of Israel, he officially approved false prophets to function as representatives and guides to the nation of Israel.

Furthermore, King Ahab and his queen Jezebel often invited 400 to 450 prophets of Baal and prophets of Asherah to come eat and drink in celebration with them (1 Kings 18:19). Shortly after, these prophets who were often in the company of King Ahab and Jezebel, began speaking words they knew King Ahab desired to hear and guaranteed him and his army the victory in capturing the city of Ramoth-Gilead. A frequent attribute of the false prophets established in biblical history is that they were often found employed to the rich and powerful, always being careful to verbalize pleasant, affirmative, and satisfying words suitable to their employers.

Jeremiah the prophet reprimanded many counterfeit prophets who always spoke in opposition to the real message of God, confusing God's people. As God was stirring Jeremiah to warn his people about the reality of being taken captive into Babylon (because of their wickedness and sins), the false prophets were giving them messages of peace and hope when there was no serenity and expectation (Jeremiah 6:14). Instead, the false prophets preached a popular inspirational message, influencing the people, of comfort and victory against Babylon. Jeremiah grew weary of these sham leaders and their messages of deception; however, God informed Jeremiah that his people love to hear the words of these diviners because it was easy to accept, be in agreement with, and believe (Jeremiah 5:31). Although Jeremiah was a true prophet of God, the false prophets were rewarded and honored by the king while Jeremiah was tortured and cast into a dungeon (Jeremiah 38:6).

The book of Jeremiah is such an interesting and fascinating book to read because of its structure and historical setting. Jeremiah's hope of reaching Israel based on God's spoken word was translated to be a false message because God's people were unenthusiastic and uninspired to heed, accept, and comply with reality. What reality? The reality of defeat by the Babylonians (an ungodly nation) and being taken into captivity as slaves and prisoners in bondage. Jeremiah's message (divinely inspired by God) didn't sound all loving, soft, and easy to receive; therefore, it was unwanted and rejected.

It is similar to the way many of us think and rationalize in our own minds when God's written Word reflects strong and unsympathetic statements, statements of judgment and clear-cut rulings, statements that correct our current lifestyle and behaviors; then we say within ourselves, "God is a loving God; he wouldn't do something so insensitive, God accepts all people, no matter who we are, what we do, and how we live." If that was the case, what is the purpose and meaning of redemption, salvation, deliverance, and sanctification? We lower the standards and value of God's written word while heightening the god of our own imaginations, personal thoughts, and feelings. It is important to bear in mind and understand that we were made in the image and likeness of God and that image was altered because of sin.

We can no longer attempt to create new gods or idols made in the image and likeness of man as a way to justify self-righteousness. We must allow God to approve who we are and mold us into who we will become, because there will be many in this world, in our neighborhoods, at our place of employment, even in our churches and organizations, who will tell us things that make us feel good under false pretenses.

In other words, there will be countless soothsayers whose exclusive interest in you is to appease your conscience with counterfeit dreams just for the sake of your personal gain (your wealth, support, influence, sex, and power). Furthermore, after those false prophets, teachers, leaders, and people in general who inspire you with artificial promises finish draining the life out of you and your possessions, they will abandon you like an old car in a junkyard, leaving you behind like damaged cargo, while you suffer, in need of some serious physical/spiritual rehabilitation.

A biblical reference found in the book of 2 Timothy 3:13 implies the existence of corrupt and dishonest people who will go from morally wrong to disgustingly gruesome in search of those who can easily be deceived and led astray — while simultaneously deceiving themselves. This reference of scripture always reminds me of the prophet Jeremiah and his challenges with the false leaders during that period of his life; it also makes me visualize and imagine these dreadful practices in today's society (to the extreme) and the innumerable people who are ensnared in this day-by-day web of deception.

God sympathetically advises Jeremiah in Chapter 23 about the grief that lies in store for his elected leaders and shepherds who have annihilated and dispersed the very people they were obligated to love and care for, stating that instead of God's leaders showing compassion for his people and directing them to safety, his guides have deserted them – steering them down the path of ruin. God promises Jeremiah that he will judge these unfaithful shepherds and will assemble the remnants of those who chose not to be deceived.

He also promised Jeremiah that he will position them in a healthier relationship with responsible leaders and shepherds – people who will be concerned about them and be devoted to their needs, while restoring and expanding their relationship with the Creator himself.

There's an unspoken stigma in the Christian and/or religious community that utters: If someone observes immoral behaviors/dishonest practices in their leaders, they are obligated to close their eyes and become blind and silent to their irreverent activities, solely because of their title, position in the church, ministry, or organization. Furthermore, plenty of people believe they will be blessed if they conceal the unconfessed sins of these leaders, becoming mute to sinful conduct.

Now that's what you call deception, when someone believes they will be blessed through injustice and inequality (speaking as a witness). In fact, many will quote scripture passages out of context, such as the story between Moses and Miriam (Moses' and Aaron's sister). This passage of scripture is often used as a scare tactic to impart fear into the hearts of God's people, causing them to disregard and remain voiceless in retrospect of the ill behavior of their leaders. You will hear many who will quote, "You better keep your mouth off of the man of God," as if God will strike us dead for discovering and exposing ungodly practices and we forget that GOD IS TRUTH.

In the book of St. John 4, Jesus was in discussion with a Samaritan woman who sat at a particular well. Now the meaning behind this story depends upon having a general idea about the well itself. This particular well in Samaria was primarily used by married women who gathered water for their husbands and families. When Jesus saw this particular woman at the well (which indicated she was married), he asked her to bring him some water to drink.

After conversing with her, Jesus convinced this woman that He was the living waters of eternal life. When she earnestly desired to partake of this unique water, Jesus uttered these famous words: *"Go and get your husband."* Then the woman stated, *"I don't have a husband."* Jesus, being amazed with her honest response stated, *"You are absolutely right when expressing that you don't have a husband."*

Although Jesus exposed the secrets and dark areas of her life, he concluded the conversation by declaring that this Samaritan woman spoke the TRUTH – although speaking the truth may have degraded her character somewhat; she still spoke the truth, which captured Jesus' attention. Whenever truth is spoken, no matter whom it may humiliate, TRUTH always captures God's attention because that is who he is and it is impossible for him to deny himself.

In Numbers Chapter 12, Miriam was not speaking the truth, nor did Miriam speak directly against Moses, but she criticized Moses for marrying a Cushite (black) woman and attempted to justify her statements because she was a prophetess. So, Miriam was not cursed with leprosy because she stated things that were true/untrue about Moses and his behavior, but she was cursed because she believed her title and position in God granted her the right to speak in error and be justified.

Many other passages of scripture are used to cause God's people to suffer silently in fear, but if we want truth and seek Christ for it, we'll certainly get God's attention and it will be granted to us as shown in His Word. God continues to tell Jeremiah that His heart is overwhelmed and sore because His prophets have become counterfeit in their dealings, and abuse what power they have. God emphasized that He had seen His prophets who reside in Samaria demonstrate deceit and intentionally make false statements to His people in the name of Baal (the idol god) and lead His people into practicing sin.

He also cited His prophets who lived in Jerusalem (meaning the possession of peace) as being even worse than those who lived in Samaria, for they lived an adulterated life and craved dishonesty – inspiring His people in their wrongdoings and preventing them from repenting and turning away from their sins.

This is not an indictment against God's leaders, because many of God's leaders and people strive to live a life of humility and love: Love that is not merely verbal communication or in theory, but in action and genuineness (1 John 3:18); love put into practice and is authentic during good and bad times, cheerful or sad times; love that's continual and sustainable. But this is expressed toward those who assume that all men and women who preach, teach, and prophesy are sent by God. Even those who appear to be doing great things for God, holding a high position in the church, and extremely wealthy, if it's by deceit, may not be God-sent. As the scripture states in the book of 2 Corinthians 10:18:

"It is not the man or woman who praises and commends themselves is approved, honored, and accepted by God; but it is the person whom the Lord endorses and entrusts."

Christ has stated repeatedly in the New Testament scripture that the greatest among His people shall become the servant to others. Preaching from a pulpit does not constitute serving because the Bible can be read from anywhere, including your own home; furthermore, serving is much more than standing behind a pulpit or platform. The act of serving is simply supporting other people's necessities and, at times, putting those requests before our own needs. The act of serving requires more than washing someone's feet once a year; it's a daily and perpetual performance (starting with those in your own family).

It's an unfortunate truth to make known, but not every preacher, pastor, or leader who appears on television (beloved and highly respected) is a follower of God directly under the control and influence of Christ. In reading the qualifications required to hold the office of a bishop/elder, found in the book of 1 Timothy 3, I cannot find anywhere in these passages of scripture that wearing fine clothing, possessing spiritual gifts, being eloquent in verbal communication with the ability to influence others, or standing before people with a bible in your possession makes you automatically eligible to embrace the office of a pastor, bishop, elder, or leader.

As we observed in the days of Jeremiah, not everyone who appeared before God's people, even those previously recognized as God's prophets/leaders, were divinely inspired by the Spirit of the Living God to speak on His behalf.

In the New Testament, Jesus warned His disciples to be very cautious when all people verbalize only good things about you, as their ancestors did, by speaking well with high hopes about the false prophets (Luke 6:26). He also advised His disciples to beware of false prophets who outwardly appear as leaders/followers of Christ (in sheep's clothing), but in reality are similar to starved wolves on the hunt, only seeking to overwhelm and consume your soul with deceitfulness and fraudulence (Matthew 7:15).

When speaking of the signs of the times and the end of the age in the book of Matthew 24: 1-5, His disciples asked him for a precursor to recognize when the end is near. This was Jesus' initial response:

"Be watchful and observant that no one mislead you by deceiving and leading you into error. For many will come in (on the use of my name) stating that "Jesus is Lord" and yet lead many astray.

In this particular set of scriptures, Jesus was not referring to the false prophets and the false Christs who will arise and deceive many, as found in Matthew 24:11, 24, but in this sequence of scriptures Jesus was referring to those who will preach/use the name of Jesus as a way to deceive, manipulate, control, and abuse you. Jesus strongly urged His followers to be watchful and observant of these kinds of behaviors. However, if we make dutiful efforts to become more attentive to the teachings of others, our attention to detail will become insulting to some and we'll be labeled as judgmental, being tagged as those who are dangerous or argumentative, when all we were attempting to do is pursue Christ and His teachings.

The Apostle Peter reminded us that there will be false teachers in our midst who will cunningly teach destructive and immoral doctrine. While those teachers/leaders will praise the Lord Jesus Christ, their teachings will be in opposition to Christ's teachings, in defiance of salvation as an outright denial against the God who delivered them and saved their souls. And the sad thing is, the passage of scripture goes on to say that "many" will follow those wicked and deceptive teachings; and, in their self-indulgence, these false leaders will make up clever lies to get hold of your money (2 Peter 2:1-3).

My question to you is, will you be one of those who will follow God's written word at all cost? Or will you be one who will trail the crowds being dazzled by an influential leader, although his/her teachings may be in direct contrast to God's Word? I remember talking to a pastor in Virginia, and we were discussing a certain subject topic. In our conversation the revelation about a passage of scripture was unveiled as we both looked up certain words using biblical dictionaries, etc. To my surprise, this certain pastor appeared to be dismayed. I asked him, "What was going on and why was he looking so puzzled". His reply was "Man, although I now clearly understand this passage of scripture, I really enjoyed the way I previously preached this message with its former comprehension."

He then concluded that he would maintain his prior teachings with the incorrect interpretation and meaning, just because it sounded much better and was easily embraced. To this leader, the style of his preaching had a greater weight than the truth of his message. I always pondered within myself, "What doctrinal truths are being forsaken and lessons being taught erroneously for the sake of his style, technique, and performance?"

Unfortunately, he is still the senior pastor and minister of a congregation in Virginia, and as the scripture taught us earlier, many shall follow his ways. Why? Because few people are willing to challenge the genuineness of God's Word. It is much more convenient to go along with the program and become a drone than to stand up for the reality of God's written expression and be mistreated by those in Christian leadership or religious leaders.

My prayer for him is that he gains a hunger and thirst after righteousness (not perfection, because none of us can measure up to existing in this life without error, but we all can choose to operate in right standings). For the beloved John informed us in the book of 1 John 4:1 that we should not believe everyone who declares to speak by the Spirit of God, but test the spirit of the message (through investigation and analyzing of God's Word) to see whether they speak by the permission or omission of God, as John concluded with this thought, *"For there are many false prophets in the world."*

In several places found in biblical history, the Apostle Paul makes an appeal to the church and warns us to watch out for and stay away from those who would keep God's people in opposition of each other by purposely disrupting people's faith as a result of "teaching things contrary" to sound (proven and factual) doctrine, explaining to us that those leaders who practice this behavior do not truly serve the Lord Jesus Christ but serve their own interests (appetites) by using compelling speeches and gleaming words to deceive the hearts of God's innocent people (Romans 16: 17-21).

I was once part of several congregations where, if you didn't agree with or wholeheartedly follow the direction of the leadership, they turned church members against you, even those of your very own household. I state to those who are persuaded by this tactic (of influence and control) not to allow anyone to have that much power and supremacy over you, unless it is Christ, the one who died on the cross for your sins and rose from the grave for your redemption.

This book is not a tool to teach God's people how to be defiant toward leadership, but it is a tool to be used to help God's people manage their own souls by learning to be obedient to God. God does not require His people to be obedient to the voice or command of a leader, or to be faithful to those leaders' every call, but to be obedient to Christ's teachings and His way of living as we freely yield ourselves servants for Christ's sake.

So, whether people agree/disagree with our leaders, we as God's people should never be drawn to take sides by division and dissention, loving and unifying only with those who love and unify with our leaders while simultaneously separating from those (especially God's chosen people) who may not always agree with or view things the way our pastor/leader sees it. In the Bible, when the Apostle Paul and Barnabas had a strong disagreement, found in the book of Acts 15: 36-40, so physically compelling that they were forced to separate from each other, Paul did not write a letter to all the churches established in Asia Minor, urging them to stay away from and part from Barnabas; neither is it recorded that Barnabas taught people to detach from and divide from Paul because of their disagreement.

So why are we taught the opposite? Why are God's people being taught (verbally/nonverbally) to love and unify only with those who love and unify with the organization and the leadership, and being taught to abort relationships and separate from those who have a misunderstanding, or those who disagree with their organization/leadership? We are all aware that the church "as an organization and a people" possesses many flaws (me included); therefore, it is in our own best interest that we serve and honor the one who has no blemish and praise the one who has mastered the art of flawlessness – none other than our true Lord and Savior Jesus Christ – God manifested in the flesh as our perfect example of human behavior and Christian maturity.

The Apostle Paul reiterated in the book of Galatians 4: 17-18 how false teachers with corrupt intentions will strive to win your favor and divide you from others so you will only pay attention to them. As we conclude with the importance of recognition and understanding of the tactics of false prophets, teachers, and leaders, I would like to point out a few more interesting points found in Jeremiah's period of time. God strongly emphasized to Jeremiah how false prophets will fill people's hearts with futile hopes and dreams.

How many times have we heard someone prophesy to someone else about becoming a millionaire, or prophesy about a certain future spouse, house, car, or career, but how many of these empty dreams have we seen truly come to pass or remain fruitful (because we can force things to be, although they may not have been intended – and in those cases the end results are generally futile)?

How many underprivileged people have we seen in the church who have received a word of prophecy about becoming millionaires and that prophecy came to fruition, other than those who serve in leadership? In addition, how many marital relationships have we seen that were put together through prophecy end up in divorce, destroying a family? Where are the numerous examples found in biblical settings where Jesus and His prophets took the time to prophesy to people about becoming millionaires, etc., with no purpose to shadow the prophecy?

I fully comprehend the notion that by serving the Lord he will and has supplied our needs accordingly; however, I'm still searching the Word of God for the abundance of prophecies concerning material possessions guaranteed to all Christians. There will be many who can customize the scriptures out of context in an effort to mislead us, but if we initiate looking up biblical definitions and applying them to the appointed dispensation of that period in time, we may not conclude with the same outlook as before.

As God told Jeremiah in verse 16 of Chapters 23, these false prophets and leaders construct imaginative fantasies based on impulse but do not speak for HIM. In fact, God even informed Jeremiah that countless of these prophets and leaders have not been in His presence to really hear Him speak; however, they are enthusiastic and eager to tell people that God has given them a word for their lives, when the Lord says he has given them no message to recite.

Furthermore, God stated to Jeremiah that if they (these prophets and leaders) had truly taken the time to hear HIM, they would have spoken HIS true words which would have turned His people away from their evil ways and deeds. See, God would rather tell His people about a life-changing experience that would impact them eternally than a material occurrence that would only change His people temporarily.

Yet in the church, the majority of these messages and words are geared toward materialistic things with a temporary impact that focuses only on the carnal nature of life. These are the kinds of lessons found written in the Word of God which, if we study them and stand in agreement with them, we'll stand divided and alone in various organizations and ministries (not all ministries but, yes, the majority of them are ensnared in this prosperity doctrine aimed at keeping certain elected individuals and their entire offspring flourishing, successful, and prosperous).

I implore everyone, as readers, not to interpret my words as furious, but I am exposing and enlightening you on the disheartening realism that occurs in ministries worldwide, which is indeed difficult to swallow; but it's time to grasp things as they truly appear. God makes this appeal to Jeremiah and states, "Doesn't my word burn like fire?" and, "Is it not like a mighty hammer?" Yet today, it appears that God only gives "feel-good messages" with no thought of correcting, building, and establishing His people. God goes on to say that these prophets He stands against steal messages from each other with claims that these messages were divinely inspired and they continue to induce His people with imaginary dreams that ultimately lead to sin as people persistently trust and receive these statements, (Jeremiah 23:29-31).

I leave you with this thought: How do you know whether or not you are following God or following someone who appears to be godly or godlike? Jesus stated in a parable found in the book of St. John 10: 3-5 that His sheep hear, pay attention to, and are familiar with His voice (the voice of the Lord and Savior Jesus Christ, captured and transpired in written documentation for us to read and discern for ourselves, with the assistance of the Holy Spirit that lives within us and within His chosen leaders). Christ continues to state that His sheep will not follow (on any account) the voice of a stranger (strange doctrines and teachings) but will run far away from illusory messages and smooth talk/speeches because they (His sheep) can discern the difference between Christ's words and the voice/words of deception and manipulation.

The Bible notes in the book of 1 Chronicles 10: 13-14 that King Saul (the king of Israel) died because he was unfaithful to the Lord, he failed to obey the Lord's commands, and he consulted a medium instead of asking the Lord for guidance. God alone and His Word are the standards by which everything should be judged and measured...but that depends on you and me.

CHAPTER 4

AVOID CONTROLLING SPIRITS

Jesus told His disciples in the book of Matthew 20: 25-26 that the leaders and high-ranking officials of the Gentile nation dictated their supremacy over them; and their most influential leaders (men, to include women) oppressed the people under their subjection, becoming oppressors/lords over them. However, Jesus made this profound statement: "That type of domineering behavior shall not be practiced by you (God's chosen leaders), but whoever wishes to be great among you and whoever it is that desires to be looked upon as primary, essential, or important in the kingdom of God, must initially become a servant to His people." What's so amazing about this sequence of scriptures is the brilliant illustration Jesus painted regarding how His leaders should exercise God's authority and power, as opposed to how others use their clout to govern/rule people.

Jesus laid this foundation, saying that in the kingdom of God the greater you are or aspire to become, the more you must serve and devote yourself to the service of people. Jesus, who is the greatest manifestation of God that eyes have ever seen or ears have ever heard, made this statement in verse 28 of this same chapter: He (Jesus) did not come into this world to be served (people fulfilling His necessities and attending His every wish), but He came to meet the provisions of others and to become a ransom for many to set His people free from the bondage and control of sin.

As I was writing this section of the book, my wife overheard me reading the information out loud and asked me this question: What has happened that we (God's people) have gotten so far off track and out of place? And my main response was: Man-made religion! The order/rule of the church or organization has become more superior and is esteemed to be of greater importance than the credence and acceptance of the Word of God. The ideology of this is: If I become connected to a church, religion/spiritual group, or organization (as to the name, popularity, size, location, religious conviction, or famous leader), and follow the rules established by these assemblies, then I'll automatically be in right standings with God.

The word "religion," according to several biblical sources, is defined as a belief in and reverence for God or some supernatural power that is recognized as the creator and ruler of the universe; an organized system of doctrine with an approved pattern of behavior or practice with a prearranged form of worship. If we recognized God in Christ as the only Supreme Being and savior of our souls, then true religion would remain pure and untainted.

However, if we follow the credibility of religion as seen through eyes of humanity (whether with good or bad intentions) then religion becomes contaminated, stained, and damaged. James, the disciple of Christ, described religion as: "Pure religion (which is described in outward acts or external duties of his/her faith) that is unblemished in the sight of God the Father is this: to help, care, and support those orphans/widows who are in need (becoming a servant) while simultaneously maintaining your personal relationship with God and refusing to be corrupted or enticed by worldly pleasures that are contrary to the will of God (remaining unblemished).

One of the greatest examples found in the Word of God that exemplifies man's religion as supremely dominant and held in higher regard over truth (which is the essence and core of Christ) is found in the book of St. John 9 – the story about the blind man whose sight Jesus restored. The blind man's parents were part of a religious group called the Pharisees. Many of these Pharisees (also known as a religious and political party in Palestine in earlier biblical history) insisted that the law of God be observed (as the scribes interpreted it and for their special commitment to keeping old laws and rituals in purity) and did not give acceptance to Christ, to His Word, nor His teachings. In fact, because Christ's teaching exceeded (but not excluded) the old laws and rituals, all those who followed the authority of the Pharisees were subjected to the same objections against Christ and stood in opposition to the power and value of His Words.

When the blind man's parents were asked by these Pharisees how their son received his sight, although knowing the truth, they were terrified to proclaim Jesus as the healer, for fear they would be removed from the synagogue. (The Jewish leaders had already agreed that if anyone confessed that Christ was the son of God, the redeemer to humanity, they were to be immediately expelled from the organization.)

In today's society, truth is manipulated and devaluated, while church, religion, and organizational rules are inflated and integrated –

and if we don't follow these rules and regulations, regardless of what the Word of God and truth suggests, in a variety of circumstances we will be banished, removed, or expelled from these organizations. Then, if we continued to question their self-proposed guidelines in contrast to what the Bible states, oftentimes leadership will make a public spectacle out of us through verbal abuse and ridicule, finding fault in everything we attempt to achieve while openly revealing our weaknesses (shared in confidence), leaving us embarrassed and confused – so much so that the saints will not question their actions, but will agree with the abuser's judgment. Furthermore, there will not be many who will come to the aid of the mistreated/abused individual but rather will remain silent.

I was joined to a congregation, which I discussed earlier, where you had to ask permission of the pastor to do anything, all under the guise of communication. If you wanted to go on vacation, you had to get the pastor's consent. If you wanted to visit your mother's or grandmother's church, you first had to get the pastor's approval.

If you wanted to buy a car or a house, or if you wanted to do anything, you had to get the authorization of the pastor – and woe unto you if you didn't get his permission prior to making any life decisions. Christ did not instruct His leaders of Christian faith to become miniature gods in His stead to control and have dominion over the lives of His people, as a king would regulate and dominate the lives of his subjects and kingdom. The Bible does support the importance of counsel, in which counseling is more suggestive than definitive; but an abundance of stories found in the Bible protest the ideology of control (other than under the control of the Almighty or the Holy Spirit).

The Bible illustrates in the book of Acts 8:9-10 that a man named Simon lived in Samaria for many years and was well known there as a great sorcerer. Many people idolized and followed him, took his counsel and advice, and declared him to be great, asserting that Simon's ability was directly sourced from the power and authority of God. For many years Simon captivated the people with his magic, putting them under his spell and control. As the story continues, this man Simon accepts Christ as His savior through the preaching of the apostles.

When we get rescued from sin through salvation and accept Christ as Lord of our life, we cannot continue operating and living in the same unhealthy manner as beforehand. We must humble ourselves and sanction God to make and mold us into the person He has ultimately purposed us to be, from the foundation of the world. When athletes, movie stars, or anyone who was once famous in the world and was formerly looked upon as great - receive the gift of salvation, although thankful and grateful for God's mercy, many of them struggle with no longer being the center of attention and having an extensive fan club. Eventually, they discover a way to become the reel of highlights once again, negating humility in the sight of God.

When Simon received salvation, he lost the attention and control of the people, because for the first time, the people of Samaria witnessed the true power of God. However, when Simon observed the apostles laying hands on the Samaritans, many of them awestruck as the power of the Holy Spirit resonated through them, Simon offered the apostles money for the ability to lay hands on people and become the center of attention again as in times past.

When God uses mankind to showcase His power and authority, it is never intended to be displayed for man's glory (for prestige and reputation), but always in reflection of God and the Lord Jesus Christ. Today, too many Simons are in the church, spellbinding and gripping God's people with attraction and fascination, whether through spiritual gifts obtained through the power of God, or whether through some other type of supernatural experience.

As we observed earlier in the book of Acts 3, when the Apostles Peter and John ministered to the lame beggar who sat daily at the gate called "Beautiful," and this beggar received healing FROM GOD to walk, through the assistance of His apostles, Peter noticed that the people of God, who witnessed these events as they stood in the temple, began looking at Peter and John as being superhuman and phenomenal because God chose to display His power through them. However, when Peter observed how the people began giving him and John credit for this miracle, rather than giving honor to God for His power, Peter made these astonishing statements beginning in verse 12, declaring:

"Why are you all staring at us as though we had made this man walk by our own power or godliness?", then Peter continued, *"Through faith in the name of Jesus, this man was healed...."*

Peter had the opportunity to make his name great, to become well known and recognized as a great healer, and to take credit for the power of God, which would have eventually brought him wealth, fame, and fortune; however, he rejected it and made Jesus and only Jesus the center of attention.

Where is that same tenacity today, where the emphasis of Christianity is chiefly centered on Jesus and not His leaders/followers? Where is that same persistence today, where Christianity is showcased in the Word of God and not the name of a church, organization, or denomination? Where is that same drive today, where Christianity's prominence is focused on the health of others and not the wealth of people?

The Apostle Paul made this statement to the church (the people, not the building – the called-out ones, not the stationary brick-and-mortar ones) as found in the book of Galatians 3:10:

"Foolish Galatians, who hath bewitched you, that ye should not obey the truth, before whose eyes Jesus Christ hath been evidently set forth, crucified among you?"

Bewitched is defined as "something or someone who is thrown out of position or displaced; to amaze, to astonish, to throw into wonderment; to be out of one's mind, beside one's self, or insane; to cause a person or a thing to keep his or its place, and to uphold or sustain the authority or force of anything."

So, if we insert the definition of the word bewitched in the passage of scripture, Paul's question to the people of God in Galatia would read something like this:

"Oh, silly Galatians, who or what has thrown you out of position or displaced you; who or what has amazed, astonished, or thrown you into wonderment; who or what has caused you to be out of your mind, beside one's self, or insane that you should not obey the truth, before whose eyes Jesus Christ hath been evidently set forth and crucified among you?"

Many people believe that as long as they attend the church building and do everything they are told – whether good or bad – that they are doing the will of God, or are in right standings with Him. Nevertheless, Peter, the servant of Christ and eyewitness of many of His accounts, later stated in the book of 1 Peter 5:2, as a forewarning and regulation to the leaders and spiritual directors of the church – to ensure sincere care for God's people – not leading by cruelty, intimidation, oppression, or restriction; but enthusiastically and gladly; not disgracefully motivated by the compensation and proceeds from serving in the office, but willingly and freely – not by being a tyrant, rigid, or an authoritarian but as replicas and illustrations of Christian living.

When leaders are directing people's lives in contrast to the Word of God, they (the people) are not in a meaningful relationship with God. It is not God's leaders who we should stand in fear and awe of; but the Spirit and Power of God himself, as exemplified though His already proven and tested written documentation. Respect and love God's people to include His leaders, but worship, praise, and adore the Almighty God and him only, and if there is ever a distinction between God and His leaders (as seen and written throughout biblical history), it is NOT A SIN to take the side of the Word of God rather than the influence and control of man.

Yes, there will be repercussions when you stand in disparity (based on God's Word) against a popular, superstardom, well-praised, and respected religious leader, but remember, if God is for us, who is that person or thing that can stand against us? People will state things like, "The church is not perfect," and "The pastors and leaders are not perfect," to keep us captivated and under control. Those statements are true to some degree; however, I would like to propose this thought: Although no church or institution is perfect (meaning free from error and mistakes), there exist churches, establishments, and organizations that are mature in Christian living and are interested only in our spiritual growth and maturity. And, although no pastor or leader is perfect (meaning free from fault and slip-ups), there are pastors and leaders whose hearts are only toward seeing God's people grow and mature, with no interest in controlling what we eat, where we sleep, where we go, who we spend time with, who we're around, when to take vacations, who to talk to, who to ignore, etc., (in terms of harmless and sinless events).

The Bible states in the book of John 14:26:
"But when the Father sends the Advocate as my representative – that is, the Holy Spirit – he will teach you everything and will remind you of everything I have told you."

Furthermore, the scripture declares in the book of Ephesians 4 that the gifts of the Spirit given to the church and the leaders who were chosen to guide God's people and are solely responsible for equipping and training us for the purposes of performing God's will, who will build and make the body of Christ stronger as a whole – yoking us as one in the unity of faith and in the knowledge of Christ – becoming more mature in the Lord by growing up in the faith. Henceforth, that we be no longer be comparable to immature children tossed back and forth and blown in every direction (as the wind does) with new teachings/beliefs by individuals whose mere goal is to swindle, trick, and deceive us with lies so clever they sound like the truth, as a way to control and manipulate our lives.

It's time for us to grow spiritually as Christians in the knowledge of God through His Word and serve in the body of Christ as the Lord's freemen/freewomen – servants to the most High God, freely breaking away from every form of bondage, whether person, place, or thing. Personally, I continue to serve under another, as I remain a servant to others: servant to my family, to any sister, brother, father, or mother (spiritual or carnal); but now I serve with pure motives and a biblical comprehension in perpetuating the good news of the gospel of Christ.

CHAPTER *5*

THE ESSENCE OF SALVATION

Nowadays, salvation is a broad term with various meanings. For some, it means to be associated with famous spiritual leaders or attend the most popular religious groups or Christian organizations. To others, it means the deed or appearance of being good. Salvation is more than just accepting Christ as our personal savior (the act of acceptance is simply related to being born again). The enactment of salvation is a continual process in which we choose to allow God to rescue us from the influence and control of sin that leads to (natural/spiritual) damage and destruction. This is a very interesting and important topic that is discussed infrequently; in fact, as others topics, when was the last time you heard "the message of salvation" shared, taught, or preached, other than the altar call? The word salvation appears from the book of Genesis to Revelation over 40,000 times in diverse translations; yet, many of us have never heard the message verbally, or maybe heard it only once. I'm always pondering within myself why this important biblical topic is uncommonly referenced. We may have heard or do hear more teachings citing money than we do regarding salvation, but the word money only appears from the book of Genesis to Revelation a little over 123 times.

Rather, we teach, preach, and believe that salvation is giving ten percent of our finances, salvation is coming to church (brick and mortar), salvation is being wealthy, or salvation is simply being loyal and dedicated to a person or an organization; however, the true emphasis of salvation is silenced. Salvation is a term that's defined by circumstances relating to deliverance, liberation, or simply the action of breaking away from and is commonly affixed with the declaration of "change." Change is an expression that coincides with the act of growing up, renewing, and exchanging, transforming, and converting: giving a different form, appearance, position, course or direction; to replace with another.

In the Old Testament, the word salvation is sometimes referred to as deliverance from danger and from the bondage of oppression, but salvation finds its deepest meaning in the spiritual realm of life. Man's universal need for salvation is one of the clearest teachings of the Bible and is visibly demonstrated when mankind was removed from the Garden of Eden: Man's life was marked by strife and difficulty, with an increase of corruption and violence.

One of the first acts of salvation found in the Bible was when God saved Noah and his family, preserving the life of animals then washing away the sins of the whole world by rain that flooded the entire planet. Noah and his family became the origin of another chance for mankind and was viewed by the Apostle Peter as a pattern in which full salvation is received in Christ (1 Peter 3:18-22). Throughout biblical history, there were many religious rituals and customs used as a way of atonement to restore the relationship between God and humanity; but these ceremonial observances fell short of their designed purposes as civilization was being prepared for the true source of its salvation which was reached and fulfilled by the death, burial, and resurrection of Christ.

Salvation is much more than just a simple confession or acknowledgment of Christ. It is a repetitive evolution of change guided, produced, and directed by the Word of God – which is the power and antidote to life but the kryptonite to weaken sin. The word sin relates to an offence or an act of disobedience that violates or transgresses against the law/knowledge of God, which also means missing God's mark, whether it is from the inward state and habit of the soul or the outward conduct of the life. The word sinner speaks of someone who (without conviction) habitually and routinely breaches or violates the divine law of God. The person who falls short to the act of sin could be anyone (the saint as well as the sinner).

The Bible tells us: "For we all have sinned and do come short of the glory of God." However, someone who has been born again should not be a customary offender who lives in noncompliance with God's heavenly ways. The book of 1 John 2:3-6 tells us:

"This is how we may discern (through experience) that we are coming to know/understand the ways of God: if we keep (bear in mind, observe, and practice) His teachings (precepts, commandments) whoever acknowledges that they know Christ (who is the image of the invisible God) but fails to practice and conform to His divine teachings and way of life is a liar, and the Truth [of the Gospel] is not in him.

However, those who routinely observe, treasure, and put into practice His Word (who bears in mind His guidelines and makes a valiant effort to comply with His message in its entirety), truly in them has the love of and for God been perfected (reached maturity). By this we may perceive that we are in Him. Furthermore, whoever states that he abides in Christ ought to walk and conduct himself (as a personal debt) in the same way in which He walked and conducted Himself."

Although we are not perfect (in the manner of being errorless), we must have the heart and desire to please God while in pursuit of him. I repetitively acknowledge that I can't teach perfection (flawlessness) because in this body of sin we cannot presently live a faultless life; however, I can teach and expect maturity because God has appointed every believer the ability to reach and strive toward spiritual maturity. The capability to reach a level of spiritual maturity is not based upon the longevity of a person's belief in Christianity nor the outward acts of religious behavior; but it is initiated when we truthfully and honestly allow God to purify our consciences from our corrupt nature (which has kept us oppressed and burdened with guilt) and lifeless observances to accept and practice His new way of living.

We must always commit to memory that God's ways are higher and better than our ways, and His thoughts are much more advanced and superior than our thoughts, and whatever our heart desires must be aligned with His will and purpose for our lives (it is not that God is supposed to align himself with the thoughts and cravings of our heart, but our desires be aligned with God's heart).

It is easy to follow the desires of our own heart then call it God's heart. Proverbs 21:2 informs and warns us that every way of a man/woman seems right in his/her own eyes, but the Lord evaluates and tests their hearts. Spiritual maturing is dependent upon change and the process of change is not simple. At times we wrestle with God in an attempt to maintain parts of our old identity prior to salvation.

One of my favorite biblical stories that demonstrate this sometimes difficult but necessary process is the life of Jacob as found in the book of Genesis chapter 25:21 through chapter 32. From birth, Jacob was a man who clutched/grabbed things that did not belong to him, or seized things before his appointed time. When he was born, being a twin, he latched on to his brother's heel because his brother (Esau) was born first, which meant he was the sole inheritor and beneficiary of his father's (Isaac) possessions, also referred to as "Esau's birthright."

The birthright was a right, privilege, or possession to which a person, especially the firstborn son, was entitled to by birth in biblical times. In Israel, as well as the rest of the ancient world, the firstborn male child enjoyed a favorite position that included a double portion of his father's assets upon death; in addition, the firstborn child's benefits included a special blessing from the father and the privilege of leadership of the family.

The inheritance rights of the firstborn were protected by law, so the father could not give his benefits to a younger sibling. However, possession of the birthright could be lost or stolen. Although God's blessings were on Jacob's life, he envied his brother Esau (while still in the womb of his mother, Jacob clutched Esau's heel as Esau was being born first). Jacob longed for the birthright privileges and his father's love and he was determined, in the span of his lifetime, to unseat Esau's birthright and secure it as his own. Then one day, as shown in the book of Genesis 25:29, Jacob succeeded in procuring (through exploitation) his brother's birthright, because his brother was in a desperate situation and moment in life. Jacob had what Esau needed to sustain his existence and instead of Jacob aiding his brother's necessities freely, he purposely preyed on his brother's extreme desperation/weak point in life – giving Esau what he needed (at that time) in exchange for his birthright.

Although many can argue that Esau was foolish in giving away his birthright, I would like to convey a different view of this story. If your brother or sister came to you with a desperate need, let's say they needed a thousand dollars to pay their rent/mortgage and you had the money to give, would you freely give it to them or would you bargain with them and ask for the rights to their children or spouse?

See, during biblical times, a person's name had significant meaning and Jacob's name meant heel-holder or supplanter – which also means to unseat, oust, dethrone, or overthrow. From birth Jacob wanted to dethrone Esau's birthright more than Esau desired to give it away. Although Jacob's grandfather was Abraham and his father was Isaac, men who had breathtaking associations with God, Jacob had to become acquainted with God for himself. The successes of his lineage could not be automatically transferred to him through his family's bloodline.

Salvation cannot be acquired exclusively through the success of other people, places, and organizations. Salvation and change must come through your personal relationship with the Creator of life. Over the course of Jacob's life, he gained understanding that he had swindled his brother. Later in life, he himself was misled numerous times by his wives' father (Laban), who defrauded Jacob's earnings over a 20-year span of labor by rarely paying him what he had been promised. Jacob grew weary of that lifestyle and behavior, and on one particular day in his life, he was left alone.

Jacob yearned for something different, and in the book of Genesis Chapter 32:24, he met someone who appeared radiant and superior, a man (other translations describe this man as an angel of God) who was greater in stature and figure. When Jacob saw this person, he latched on to him and would not physically release him, but wrestled with this man all night in hopes of receiving approval – which also means a blessing. When this man saw that Jacob was unwilling to release him, he touched Jacob's hip – pulling it out of its socket – which caused Jacob to (physically) walk differently.

This encounter with God changed Jacob's spiritual outlook and his bodily appearance (in terms of his new limp, which symbolized his new walk with God). Jacob never looked the same again. Jacob later described his encounter in the book of Genesis 32:30 as seeing God face to face with his life being preserved. When Christ truly touches our life, He creates and demands a change both spiritually and physically (throughout the course of our natural lives); everything about us should change, including the way we live and, as shown in this story, although change comes through a process of time, our desire to have something spiritually greater and better than ourselves should always be present. God not only changed Jacob's life, but he also he changed his name.

In the book of Genesis 32:27, when Jacob was asked about his name, his response was pivotal. Jacob did not respond by saying that he was the grandson of Abraham/the son of Isaac (for spiritual pride or appreciation), he was real with God and responded that his name was Jacob, meaning that he was a supplanter, someone who rode on the heels of others. Because of his genuineness, humility, and honesty with the Almighty, God changed his name from Jacob (a heel-holder, supplanter, and trickster) to Israel (meaning a prince with God).

When a person chooses Christ as their Lord and Savior, the titles and names we were known by should change (pimp, killer, whore, slut, etc.) because our new walk with God will demand so. Salvation changes us from who we used to be known, identified, or recognized into whom God is forming or shaping us to become. However, we must be willing to unseat and oust our past (including previous prideful accomplishments). True salvation creates desperation and a hunger to become more like Christ, lessening the craving for worldly attention, admiration, fame, or fortune – an American idol (even in the church). The Bible enlightens us about this great salvation and states that it teaches us certain things. As described in the book of Titus 2:12, salvation has appeared to humanity and instructs us to refuse ungodliness and worldly lust, admonishing us to live prudently (with common sense and godly wisdom), honorably (in all manner of behavior and dealings), and godly (in devotion to the Living God) in this present world.

The Bible clearly points out that Salvation (deliverance) is a process that includes the day-after-day practices of repentance/forgiveness that leads to change. When Christ saved us, he immediately delivered us from the penalty of sin – which was eternal death; and upon his ultimate appearance, He will deliver us from the presence of sin prior to the final judgment/conclusion of this world. But for now, God is continuing to deliver us from the power/authority of sin that plagues and governs our lives. The Bible tells us that after we accept Christ into our lives; we must allow the Spirit of God to control our mind, which leads to a prosperous life and peace. However, we must be willing to let go of our sinful nature, which leads to destruction.

If we choose to yield ourselves under the power of sin, then we become a servant to it, and if we live (habitually/continuously) by the cravings and delight of sin, we will eventually lose hope in Christ spiritually, as it will become evident in our natural lives – which could lead to spiritual and physical deception (Romans chapters 8 and 12). Oftentimes, when people read the book of Romans, especially Chapter 8, there is a sense among readers that there is no commitment to righteous living or behavior on their part, that the Spirit of God will force a life of righteousness upon us while simultaneously shunning darkness out of our lives. However, obedience is a choice and the scriptures warn us that if we continually surrender/yield ourselves to sin, we becomes servants to it and we become slaves to whatever we obey – whether that be to sin, which leads to death or whether that be obedience which leads to righteousness (right doing/living/standing) with God (Romans 6:16).

The word "if" is described as a term that suggests possible circumstances or imagined situations that may or may not happen based on the direction of choices – and the Bible is full of "ifs" and "choices", which are dependent upon you and me. God is perpetually faithful; but the same cannot be stated about us (thank God for his tender mercy).

Again, the Apostle Paul informs the Gentile believers living in Rome that those who are abiding by the guidelines of the flesh; catering to the appetites and impulses of their carnal nature cannot please or satisfy God or be found acceptable to Him. We know the power of God is infinite and His Word is immeasurable, but choosing and accepting HIM is more than just a confession of faith (through lip service and attending a building we now call the church); it is a binding relationship that costs us our entire life. The scripture tells us that sin entered the world through man, and through sin death emerged. Death (both spiritually and physically) is the permanent stain for all mankind; but Christ came and presented us with hope by exchanging His righteous life for our death sentence, offering us both spiritual and eternal reconciliation for all humanity through His death. Christ took our death and gave us His life so all who choose to live might no longer live to and for themselves, but live to and for Him who died and was raised again for our sake. If we accept His life, then it is His life we must live and not our own.

The requirements for salvation are not based upon the ability to sing in the choir, to preach or teach a bible lesson, or how much money we can give to a person and organization, becoming rich or becoming a faithful servant to a pastor, leadership, or association. Salvation is doing His will on this earthly realm as predestined in the heavenly realm, to accomplish His already designed will for our life as it is already preordain in Heaven. We must be changed, be delivered, be salvaged/saved from the power of bondage and control of sin, allowing the Holy Spirit to change our current reflection on earth to the appearance and image as predetermined in Heaven. This may take a lifetime to accomplish.

We endure life's disappointments, heartaches, troubles, and persecution as witnesses for Christ's sake (not by self-incrimination) with a promise of a better hope. We relinquish, or are supposed to relinquish, our old nature (worldly achievements, image, or clout), our selfish status as permanent citizens on this earth, with the mindset of being eternally with the Lord, Although we are in this world and receive compensation/appreciation for what we offer to this world, these things should be worn like a loose garment, ready to fall off; although we are in this world, we as Christians are not supposed to be of this world – meaning continually being shaped/molded by its carnal nature but governed by the power of the Word of God reflecting the life of Christ.

Christ was born and lived on this earth. He was a carpenter by trade, as described in the book of Mark 6:3. He had a chosen, earthly father, a natural mother, brothers and sisters, and he abided by the laws of the land. However, he didn't live like others lived. He existed according to the Creator of life and was governed by the Word of God. Although he accomplished many things and did numerous good deeds, he served God.

True Christianity is not popular when wholesome, in its unpolluted and untainted state – when it's lived as God intended it to be. True Christianity is not about winning Grammys, Oscars, or Humanitarian awards, nor is it about the popularity of a person, place, or institution. In fact, Christianity in its uncontaminated condition looks ridiculous and unintelligent: living your life by faith in something you cannot see or touch – having not seen, yet we love, having not grasped, yet we believe. Christianity does not endeavor to be like or imitate the world, but strives to be a beacon of light and hope in this dark and gloomy realm that is perpetually increasing in corruption and brutality, wickedness and unimaginable evil.

CHAPTER **6**

PURE FAITH

Faith is like a power tool that if taught/used inaccurately can build a temporary emotional high that eventually concludes with a ton of unproductive and ineffective results. It is like purchasing a brand-new car without tires. Although we can be extremely enthusiastic about the latest sedan and its features, without the required components that would allow this vehicle to be more efficient, the purpose of the purchase is left unfulfilled.

In today's society, faith is an expression that is often used as a catch phrase with various meanings, such as courage, belief in oneself/others/organizations, or trusting in a product/system of some sort. However, faith that is furnished by God is like a master lock that requires a three-digit combination to open, releasing the benefits it treasures. Furthermore, in the realm of Christianity, what is the true meaning of faith? How do we acquire faith and maintain it? Lastly, how do we grow and mature our faith?

The relationship we create with God through our salvation and acceptance of Christ is the gateway to maximizing our faith. The Bible states (Hebrews 11:6) that without faith it is impossible to please God, give him satisfaction or bring him contentment, and that those who approach God must believe he exists and is real (not just a religious experience or a creative imagination); and He will reward those who vigilantly pursue him. We must wait patiently for God to reward us and not pursue our own rewards obtained through lustful and sensual pleasures. God's rewards are not always financial or material incentives, and the essence of faith is not about believing in God for physical gratification as many portray, but more so spiritually.

God knows our human necessities and blesses us with earthly pleasures in this life, but God demands that His people thoroughly inquire about the kingdom of God, which is His righteousness, peace, and joy in our lives – the visible manifestations of His invisible and pure attributes. If these material pleasures here on earth were God's ultimate rewards, will, and purpose for His people, then there would be no need for a heavenly realm wherein the focus is not obtaining and gaining material wealth.

John the beloved, as found in the book of Revelations, does his very best in human form to share with us his spiritual vision in physical depiction: Heaven is described as a place where the streets are paved with gold and dwelling places viewed as mansions. However, the Bible clearly defines the purpose of this sin-free and righteousness place in one phase: God's reconciliation with man as man honors God in worship, adoration, and praise. Jesus makes this statement: *"Thy will be done on earth as it is (as a mirror image) in Heaven,"* and in all the passages of scriptures established in the Word of God that illustrate this awe-inspiring place called Heaven, there are no mentions of money, wealth, riches, or possessions as pertaining to man's necessity for it.

Therefore, the case can be made that it is not God's essential will for us to exclusively focus the bulk of our attention (here on earth) seeking, gathering, and storing great quantities of wealth, because these physical temporary enjoyments don't replicate His permanent and eternal will for us in Heaven. Furthermore, Jesus warns us in the book of Luke 12:15:

"To safeguard ourselves and keep free from all covetousness/materialism (the excessive desire for wealth, the greedy craving to have more) for a man's life does not consist in nor is derived from possessing a magnitude of wealth in overindulgence and beyond a man's needs."

Faith begins with our recognition and belief in God to include His unified beings. Christ is the image of the invisible God, the Spirit of God robed in human flesh who dwelt among His people. Although God chose to be clothed in human form in the person of Christ, the fullness of God's Spirit is too immeasurable and infinite to be solely contained in one single vessel or in a solitary place at one time. This is why the scriptures state that those who come to God must believe HE exists, to include HIM (His entire deity, in the appearance of the Father, Son, and Holy Spirit).

Simply, the Holy Spirit is a portion of God's Spirit given to those who believe and obey Him (Acts 5:32). The Holy Spirit is a portion of God's limitless spirit that appears as our supporter, comforter, teacher, and counselor in our lives as believers. Millions of true believers in this world have been given the gift of His Spirit because of their acceptance of Christ and their obedience of the gospel. Yet he is still one God, not a million, when we understand that God cannot be measured and has no boundaries – the supply of God's Spirit is unrestricted. In addition, it is impossible to accept God and yet deny the Son.

The Bible tells us in the book of 1 John 2:23 and 2 John 1:9 that if anyone rejects or denies the Son (Christ), he concurrently discards and refutes the Father (God) and cannot acquire one without the other; In addition, anyone who drifts away from the teachings of Christ has no relationship with God; but those who remain attentive to the words of Christ have relationship with both the Father and the Son.

Everyone has the right and opinion to accept a god or some form of religion/belief without accepting Christ, but it is impossible to accept God (the Creator of life and all things) without accepting the Son of God, who is the incarnation of the Almighty created in human form, and God cannot deny the divinity of himself in His Son. This is the initial step toward understanding pure faith and the first combination number to unlocking wholesome assurance – believing in God. Furthermore, it is vital, with all conscientiousness, that we give strict attention to the words of Christ so we can have continuous fellowship with the Father, because everyone who claims to have the Son doesn't follow his teachings.

Secondly, and probably the most misused combination number in unlocking faith is the act of hearing and believing God's (confirmed) Word. God's Word is no longer a mystery and has been plainly declared to His people. All too often, God's Word is misspoken in confusion and held in mystery to keep God's people out of sync with Him for the sole purpose of being kept beneath the constraint and restriction to the willpower of man.

Every spoken word we hear and receive outside of the already confirmed Word of God should not be acted upon until we personally seek God's heart for confirmation of any spoken word apart from His written script and learn to judge all spoken words by His all-powerful historical biblical document written and existed before all mankind. These important spiritual tips will keep us safe from deception and save us tons of heartaches while we learn to hear from God for ourselves and confirming it through His Word. I can't stress the importance of this enough, although I make a valiant attempt.

Faith has always been governed, initiated, and originated by God's Word. By faith, the world was framed and fashioned, piece by piece by God's Word, and the evidence of what is now witnessed was constructed out of things that are invisible and inconceivable to human sanity. By faith, Noah built an ark of enormous size, dry-docked on land and not in an area near the sea, because God's Word instructed him to do so. Although Noah had never seen rain before and could not fully understand the rationale of building a huge ship to house animals, he obeyed God's Word.

For faith is the substance or physical confirmation of the things we hope for, without the evidence or proof being visually seen or without the conviction of its reality (faith being the perception of what is not revealed to the senses), and by it (faith as originated by God's Word) men/women of the ancient world (our elders who lived before us) trusted in God and had heavenly experiences borne to them, leaving a legitimate legacy for us to follow.

By faith, the Apostle Peter walked on water toward Jesus, but was first given permission to come forth by the word of Christ. By faith, Abraham left his native country and his kinsman in search of a promised land in which he was destined to receive an inheritance from someone other than his native father. By faith, he traveled through desolate lands in search of a place that he himself would never obtain, but trusted in and was driven by God's Word and voice. Abraham's faith made the invisible visible and the impossible possible.

But in every area of these biblical stories, as well as the innumerable stories of faith demonstrated in the Holy Scriptures, God's Word was the foundation and institution of their actions. There are many people/Christians are walking out on unestablished faith, hoping and expecting to obtain, and are doing some of the most ridiculous things in optimism of receiving, such as giving away hundreds of thousands of dollars (in some cases their life's savings) while being promised to take delivery of millions in return, only to collect broken promises and seeds of deception. Faith is not naming and claiming something that God has not ordained for us to take hold of; it is not blabbing and grabbing something that is not destined for us to acquire.

Faith is believing in God, hearing with acceptance (His predetermined confirmed word), and the performance of His Word. Faith is not jumping off of the Golden Gate Bridge in hopes of God rescuing you just because you believe in Him, for His Word prohibits us from enticing Him by challenging His authority and abilities for personal pleasures with no productive resolutions. This reminds me of the story when Jesus was tempted by the Devil in the Wilderness, when Satan took him to Jerusalem – to the highest point of the Temple – and enticed him by stating that if he was the Son of God then jump off and order His angels to catch him. Then the Devil had the audacity to quote biblical writings out of context to lure Jesus into abusing His power and authority. However, the Word of the Lord returned to Satan in accuracy, responding with:

"The scriptures also say, 'You must not quiz or test the Lord your God."
(Luke 4: 9-12)

God's Word does not sanction us to challenge him with senseless things. But God's Word does teach us how to forgive, with the ability to forgive those actions that seem the most unforgivable, and teaches us how to love those who don't love us. These godly responses take a great deal of faith because the nature of man teaches us to love only those who adore us and hate/despise those who dislike and detest us.

It's not the real deep things of faith that pleases God, but it's an assortment of simple things that satisfy him and brings him pleasure. In reality, there is no such thing as blind faith; faith is sighted through the hearing and believing of God's Word and it's through the Word of God that faith appears. It is up to us (God's people) to hear God's confirmed word, which brings us to the third combination number that unlocks faith

– the action that follows what we both hear and believe as hearers and doers of His word. The ability to hear, believe, and obey God's Word is the difference between someone who hears about a severe storm and takes no refuge and someone who hears about that same storm but follows all precautions, taking safe haven, hearing and doing –not just hearing only. As demonstrated by many of our biblical forefathers/mothers, if we choose to hear, trust, and obey God's Word, despite our human emotions, we will mature in faith and belief, and will spiritually grow as a Christian who is truly Christ-like and not religion-driven or man-made.

Moreover, it takes matured faith to follow/trust God's written word in disagreement with others whose vision for you/your life is not God's vision, but their own – in response to fulfilling their own personal pleasures. Taking a position for biblical truth takes great faith, because the stance being made is not popular, and we may be publicly ostracized and made to look foolish, possibly making us second-guess our own faith and posture. It also takes mature faith to pursue/rely on God's Word in a society where everything is democratic, even God. If the majority of people believe God to be a certain way then that belief or way must be right and becomes the permanent way, regardless of the Word of God. To a sundry of people, the Bible is outdated and should not be used for today. Faith matures and grows when the Word of God matures and grows in us, and this can only happen when we read it, hear it, believe it, accept it, and live it. Selah!!

RELIGION VS. REALIZATION:
The True You

The willingness to change is like an undiscovered treasure, and the value of transformation is priceless. Adjustments are necessary in this Christian walk in order to sustain our faith, to endure life's hardships, to withstand troubled times, and to discover who we really are. Religion only teaches us to quote numerous scriptures that pertain to our situation, to loose those things that are bound in Heaven; while binding those things that God has freely given us to enjoy – disguising the authority of Christ as an excuse to implement human totalitarianism, dictatorship, and hypocrisy as faith and accountability, keeping us spiritually ignorant and in bondage under the spell of carnal rules, regulations, commandments, and laws. Religion also keeps us unconscious about who we really are; while at the same time, keeps us motivated in attaining the unattainable, chasing unrealistic dreams and fantasies – keeping us emotionally high.

In the book of Matthew 26:42, as Jesus enters the garden of Gethsemane, He displays the emotions of grief, distress of mind, and deep depression, because His hour had come. I thank God for the reality of what Christ exhibited – His humanity despite His divinity. Being a witness/servant for Christ is not how well we can illustrate our loyalty to a person, place, or thing (other than God himself), but the true essence of Christianity is discovering the real you – understanding your humanity despite the power of His divinity. Christ is and forever will be the only superhuman.

Many Christian believers primarily focus on possessing the outward appearance or religious forms of godliness without embracing the nature of Christianity through the gospel of Christ – which is the topmost authority of God. We say the right things, we give the impression of looking the correct way, we draw our satisfaction from attending some form of religious gatherings throughout the week; but we make no attempt in allowing God to change those sinful habits in us that hinder us from truly pleasing Him.

It's true, as we have always heard; When a person chooses to follow Christ, God is not interested in solely changing the outer perception first and foremost; but he has planted His seed within us so that we may blossom and bloom from within, which will eventually be visibly witnessed. See, we cannot fool God with our emotions and physical antics; he's not impressed because we can praise him the loudest or clap softly.

God informed the prophet Isaiah in Chapter 29:13 that His people draw close to him with their mouths and show admiration of him with their lips, but their hearts/minds are disinterested and distant from the reality of him, as their fear and reverence of Him are according to the commandants of men who learn by habitual practices without any thought to the real meaning of what they do. In the book of Matthew 15:8, Jesus quoted this same passage of scripture to the religious people of that generation, saying that the act of worship and praise in its spiritual appearance of man is worthless and empty to God because the hearts of the worshippers are secluded from God, as it is evident in their teachings and lifestyle.

Again, we cannot impress God with our outer appearance (i.e., read the Bible, attend church, and dress in fine clothing) as we can with man, but we can be real with who we are (both our good/evil nature) and make an attempt to serve God while being serviced by him. It takes great humility to understand we are nothing without the grace of God, and we are only something because of him. It also takes great humility to understand that despite the many gifts and callings of God, who transcends the lives of men/women, we are still subject to sin and error, and have a dark side about us that remains hidden from the life and light of God, which desperately needs His attention.

It takes true humility to understand that though I may be a good Sunday school teacher, I may still need help in the areas of parenting. It takes true humility to acknowledge that although I am praised for being a good usher and preacher of the gospel of Christ, I may be a dreadful spouse and a horrible friend. See, every area of our life needs special attention and our Christian religious titles do not supersede that need to improve those dark areas, and the key to change is acknowledgment of truth without denial.

As beforehand mentioned in earlier segments of this book about Jesus' encounter with the Samaritan woman at Jacob's well; He met this woman drawing water usually during the hottest time of day when no one else would be present at the well (around noontime). Throughout the course of their conversation, this woman becomes interested in what Jesus had to offer:

living water – an eternal substance to alleviate a continual thirst or need to drink and draw water (the perfect cure for thirst). When this woman desired, yearned, and requested this type of water, Jesus brings to light the unaddressed issues of her reality. This woman's emotions were at an all-time high, waiting in great anticipation for this living water that Christ was offering her, only to be delayed so she could come face to face with herself.

Again, this woman had the outer appearance and garments of a married woman who was present at the well on behalf of her husband to draw water, and she purposely came during this time of day to avoid having to acknowledge her true identity and to steer clear of the persecution that may have come her way from the other married women (who knew the true identity of this certain woman) who also drew water from this same well. Christ did not desire this woman just to be emotionally aroused, but eternally changed so after this occurrence with Him, she would not be the same as when she came. But the key to this everlasting experience was her acknowledgment of where she was in her life without justifying her reality. There is no shame as to who you are and where you are in life; the only shame is when you/I refute and reject reality. This Samaritan woman acknowledged that although she had plenty of husbands; the man she was now with is not her husband. She took note that Christ was a prophet because he saw through her disguise, and after the honest account of her life, Jesus declared her description to be true; and it is only through truth that we are made/set free.

The humanism of religion causes many to be accustomed to masquerading themselves to others for so long that eventually we become a disguise to ourselves. Our selected/elected leaders (and we as Christians) can no longer hide behind our titles, hide behind the physical structure of the church, hide behind our spiritual gifts and abilities, hide behind the bible and the capacity to quote scriptures, hide behind parents of great reputations, or the size and establishments of our ministries – yet never coming face to face with the reality of who we are. We must learn to confess our existing lust issues, sexual and nonsexual, our greed, power, and control, our substance and physical abuse issues, our anger issues, and the various other issues we could acknowledge. It is time God's people live a life of transparency, first to ourselves – in recognition of our recurrent and desperate need for Christ – then to others in declaring that whomever the Son set free is free indeed.

It is the appointed time for the Body of Christ to spiritually grow stronger and healthier, rather than enormous growth in size while extremely ineffective. In order to be successful in this quest, we, as the body of Christ, must be willing to change from our unproductive practices that have crippled Christianity and the power of its truth, and in humility be willing to recognize our inconsistencies, allowing God to modify and revolutionize our lives by the authority of His Word, and not by the influence of the World. Christianity is more than a collection of experiences – it's a test of time and endurance.

Many people have experienced Christianity at some point/time in their lives, but not too many have persevered and continued, while mounting various explanations for their abandonment toward God and Christianity. There may be plenty of genuine reasons and circumstances that would cause someone to get angry with the church establishment/church leadership and people in general, but there should be no reason for anyone to abandon Christ, the author and finisher of our faith, the creator of our souls. You've read earlier about some of my dreadful experiences in Christianity: the abandonment, the control, the manipulation, the hypocrisy, the deception, the sexual abuse, the false teachings, the cult movement, and many other things.

After discovering the reality of me, none of those things have changed my mind/opinion about Christ and God. In fact, it is the power of God that sustains me, and the knowledge of Christ that empowers me. It is the sinful nature of man in religion that blinds and abuses people; but it's the reality and understanding of the Word of God that enlightens us and brings us to greener pastures. It is a complexity because of the fact that we are supposed to have some kind of trust in our leaders/organizations; however, it's the realism that not everyone who believes in Christ is a follower of God. When you understand that, belief is more than a thought process – but it's the actions that follow the thought process.

Christ even stated in the book of Luke 6:46: "Why do you call me Lord? But you do not apply anything that I say," and it's up to believers to recognize the difference and act on what we perceive. The religion of man causes us to ignore reality while simultaneously makes us cling to deception because of influence and pressure of a person, group, or organization. It's like what Isaiah the prophet experienced: once King Uzziah died, then and only then was he able to distinguish the true Lord of His life.

What are some of those things that need to die in our life that would cause us to truly see God – His love, His freedom, His influence, His rule, and His authority? (Is it money? Sex? Power? Religion? Relationship? The influence and control of man/organizations?) It is really tough to understand and perceive who God is when we lack the perception and reality of who we are, as Christ was demonstrating with His attempt to get the Samaritan woman to embrace and come to grips with her reality and nature of life.

The Bible tells us in the book of Colossians 3:1-3: Our real life (the real you) is hidden with Christ in God and it is through your true relationship with Christ (beyond the four walls of a church, temple, or synagogue) that unfolds and brings clarity to your purpose and reality of life with God. Although Moses had the appearance of an Egyptian, it was his experience with God that unveiled his reality as a Hebrew.

When asked, "What is the greatest lesson you learned from Moses' life?" I often share those same thoughts that have been passed on to me from pulpit to platform, such as "How he suffered with God's people," and "How he was a great man of God" (which is true), but the greatest aspect about Moses' existence is rarely talked about. The biggest lesson I learned from

Moses' life is this: Moses was born a Hebrew, but for the majority of his life, he was raised as an Egyptian, learned as an Egyptian, taught as an Egyptian, treated as an Egyptian, but not a real Egyptian. All he knew about himself at this time in his life was what someone else told him (with no recognition of who he really was). But the true God we serve (not those men/women we allow to be gods in our lives) would not allow Moses to go through life being defined by someone other than the Creator.

God allowed things to occur in Moses' life: disappointments, troubles, violence, etc., just to get his attention and to make him see himself for who he really was – and not who Pharaoh said he was. God did not allow Moses to squander the rest of his life as a counterfeit Egyptian, but rather live a full life as a real Hebrew. In his case, it required him to leave a familiar place (the place he'd known all his life) for an unfamiliar place in order to continue his discovery process. Although known as "the deliverer," Moses couldn't deliver anyone out of something he was currently residing in: bondage and slavery.

Though he wasn't physically a slave, he was indeed mentally shackled. Understand, it may take years of your life, along with unpleasant situations, to get you to focus on you and not what someone says about you. It may take many years before you can discover who you really are – and only if you are willing to see you, the true you, whether good or bad.

There are three key factors to discovering the true you: willingness to accept truth, willingness to change, and time. As God began to show Moses who he really was, Moses was no longer interested in being recognized as an Egyptian. The factor of time was the next essential element in his transformation. The Moses we preach and teach about wasn't always the Moses we embrace and know. Again, the definer is God – not preachers, not teachers, not religions, not magazines or TV shows, or what the majority of society thinks – but the Creator himself. You have to allow God to help you restore your true identity, regardless of what many Pharaohs are saying about you, and you must grant yourself time to change.

One of the greatest characteristics known about the Pharaoh (meaning king) during the period and life of Moses: is that Pharaoh was the most powerful person on the face of the planet and whatever Pharaoh proclaimed about you -- is who you became regardless of who you thought you were. Unfortunately, many are living their lives as an Egyptian (mentally enslaved), though born a Hebrew (the free and true you), because Pharaoh said, "This is who you are."

As Moses' life was hidden, but made known through his relationship with God, we need a relationship with God the creator to know and understand who we are and what we are purposed for. If you have a relationship with God the Creator, then it's time to discover the true you – stripped of titles and recognition. Moses couldn't go on with the routine of life living as an Egyptian. Moses accepted himself as a Hebrew and became very proud of his heritage. The scriptures even show us that Moses chose to live and suffer with his own people rather than live like an Egyptian prince and enjoy the pleasures of life for a short time.

Do you know who you are other than what you've been told – who you are supposed to be? Many ethnicities and cultures of people make it a personal priority to understand their identity through the discovery of their heritage/origin as a people of faith and of race. The first book of the Bible, the book of Genesis, is all about ancestry. We can embrace and enjoy the ancestry of our spiritual nature as many can identify themselves as being spiritual Jews; however, that is not who God created you to become. The text of scripture found in the book of Romans 2:28, as expressed by the Apostle Paul, pertains to Jewish people not automatically becoming true believers in God simply because they are born of Jewish parents or have gone through the ceremony of circumcision.

Jewish people who become true believers are those who allow God to give them a change of heart toward Him who seeks praise from God and not from humanity. The Apostle Paul continues to express in Romans 3:29 that God is not a God of the Jews only, but to all people. So the thought that God desires all people to become spiritual Jewish believers is inaccurate and misinterpreted. (It is amazing to me to observe how people would rather embrace and identify with something or someone who disguises their true identity.)

God's desire for you/me is for us to become who He created us to be, with our own uniqueness and distinctiveness, which begins with understanding culture and origin of birth. If you were born Caucasian (or white, as culturally described), then that's who you are and that's where you begin. If you were born of African descent (or black, although there are many shades of blackness), then that's who you are and that's where you begin.

What positives have come from your race of people? What negatives have come from your race of people? The book Genesis is all about ancestry, which expresses both the good and bad of a culture/people, and whatever is broken in a culture/people, we know God can restore it/them, for He is a mender of broken pieces.

If you are of African ethnicity living in America, which I am, a lot of our history has been hidden and is not found in the traditional history books written and published through the eyes of racism. We, as black people, have been told for years that we are cursed because of the sins of Canaan, but as I was researching the book of Genesis, I learned something fascinating. After the flood, Noah planted a vineyard and partook of the fruits of his labor, which was wine produced from the grapes in his vineyard. As we all may know, the Bible said that Ham was in the tent of his father and "saw" the nakedness of his father.

Now some people may propose that Ham fondled his father, or suggest that Ham was a homosexual, but the scriptures never support that characterization. The scriptures simply state that he "saw" the nakedness of his father and then went outside and told his two brothers.
The scripture does not hint at fondling or touching, but only observing. The word "nakedness" biblically means nudity, shame, indecency, and improper behavior. No matter

what Noah may have been doing, the Bible only implies that Ham saw it. But more interesting is that when Noah wakes up out of his sleep and recognizes the sin of Ham, Noah states, "Cursed be Canaan," not "Cursed Be Ham." Ham saw the nakedness of his father, but Canaan was cursed for it.

One crucial point before I continue, you will never find anywhere in the scriptures that states, "God cursed Canaan." Many upon many generations of people have been taught and believed that God cursed Canaan, or God cursed black people, but that statement or teaching cannot be found anywhere in biblical history. Remember, Noah cursed Canaan, and not God. Now, if Noah cursed Ham, then would all of Ham's sons be cursed?

However, the Bible specifically states that Noah cursed Canaan, who was ONE of his many sons. So what's the point! CANAAN was not a BLACK MAN OR WOMAN! Canaan's name means a merchant or trader, and his decendants lived along the borders of the Mediterranean Sea, not

Africa. The Canaanites lived closer to where modern-day Israel and Jordan are today. In fact, the Bible even states that Jesus walked through Canaan and was often considered a Canaanite. Canaan was a regional place, inhabited by Abraham and his descendents and later promised to his people as a land to inherit. Again, the Canaanites were not black people of African origin. Finally, Canaan was the fourth born son of Ham. Ham had a firstborn son name Cush. Cush's name means "black, dark, and hot," and the Bible does not state that "Noah cursed Cush."

The Bible states that Cush lived in the southern region; his descendents lived in hot areas. If you follow the book of Genesis and observe the genealogy of Cush, you will notice that his descendents lived mostly in the region of Africa. Not only that, Cush had a son name Nimrod, and the Bible says that Nimrod built great cities.
Nimrod was not only intelligent but was industrious and strong as well. So, many of us who have an extraction from the African race are a strong and great people, but have been told for centuries (through history books, media, and

propaganda) that we are ill-mannered, unintelligent, and depraved. Every race of people on this planet has the good, the bad, and the ugly of their kind; but not as many are on display in public view as those with the pedigree of an African bloodline. There is so much positive about you and your people; but my question is, "Have you identified your true identity, or are you still allowing people to define you – convincing you to be something or someone you're not?"

True Christianity is about you accepting the nature of Christ; Christ revealing the power and the mysteries of God; and God restoring you/me to our true identities – a trip back to the Garden of Eden. Again, the Bible tells us in the book of Colossians 3:3 that our real lives are hidden, but they are hidden with Christ, who is in God. Discovering Christ is discovering God, and discovering God is discovering you.

CHAPTER

FINAL ANALYSIS

Real Talk

I conclude this book the same way in which the Apostle Paul ended his first letter to the church in the book of Thessalonica (Chapter 5: 21-23):

"...but test everything that is said, thought, or believed and only hold fast to those things that have proven to be good, proven to be wholesome, and proven to be truth". Furthermore, stay away from every kind of evil (whether inside or outside of your assembly) so that our God can make you holy/pure in every way possible; may your spirit, soul, and body be kept blameless until Christ returns."

These exhortations to the Thessalonian Christians were not aimed toward a particular sect, religion, or certain crowd. These general statements were inclusive of all people (even those who appear untrustworthy), not because Paul sought for us to become suspicious of everyone, but that our loyalty will always be toward God – in case that trustworthy individual gets off track and becomes indulgent in every kind of evil and we become innocent bystanders led astray by the error of mankind. Even those you find most trustworthy are capable of malicious error if they don't maintain their own faith and trust in the Lord.

Spiritual maintenance for your soul is not solely the responsibility of the leaders; you will be liable for your own soul and will be personally accountable to God on how you trusted and leaned on Him in preserving your entire spirit, soul, and body untarnished (meaning good spiritual, physical and emotional health) until His return. The greatest weapon against faith is doubt driven by fear. By far, the people of faith and religion are shackled and restricted by other people, places, and things based on the misguided self-inspiring teachings as a way to control and manipulate the hearts of the parishioners, keeping them slaves to the personal interests of others, no matter how far astray the leaders may go. The conclusion of that deadly journey (the blind leading the blind, then the sightless finally see) leads to a root of bitterness that springs up and is directed toward God (because of the abuse and pain during that murky journey) and hatred/unforgiveness toward His people/the Body of Christ. This type of conduct is generally conceived through brainwashing or what is termed as "cultural conditioning".

Cultural conditioning is the social progression in which influential authority leaders, whether political, professional, religious, or peers – to include social media; infiltrates an isolated way of thinking which controls our behavior and defines our cultural values, our beliefs, our ethical systems, and ultimately the way we perceive ourselves in the world and in the church.

Religious terminology, bias subjectivity, clever and convincing clichés are some of the many ways that cultural conditioning is subverted in our belief system in the Body of Christ. Not that we seek a perfect (errorless) body --- but we do seek a healthy (mature) one. Often times biblical scriptures are stripped of its original interpretation and significance because it (the biblical writings) are immediately interpreted to fit our purposes, private agendas, and subjects rather than seeking to authenticate its original meaning as intended through defining the meaning of all the words surrounding each passage, the historical setting, and the purposed audience in which it was initially intended for.

No one has all the correct answers or meanings: but individual study even if you are in disagreement with your favorite teacher or leader will put you on the safest path from spiritual deception and religious cultural conditioning. Critical thinking, analyzing, and questioning (such as Jesus himself displayed) is considered flagrant, insubordination, and rebellion because it collides with the cultural conditioning process: because of its freedoms and preventive measures. One of the key ingredients to avoiding bitterness toward Christianity is understanding that it's acceptable to believe and trust God's Word (in proper interpretation); over the opinions and reasonings of any leader. Although this may cause controversy and you may be ridiculed, as I stated in abundance, your relationship with Christ (according to His Word) will remain unstained and will grow in leaps and bounds.

I'm not talking about having disagreements among ourselves (although disagreement is healthy, contrary to popular belief). I'm speaking strictly toward those leaders who persistently maneuver the Holy Scriptures to accommodate self-interests under the guise of Christianity. And again, the Apostle Paul admonished the church to stay away from EVERY KIND of EVIL. You are not obligated by God to remain in a place where you are not spiritually growing.

I shared with a pastor friend of mine that he should not be upset with the people of God who decide to leave the church for whatever reason, because the reasons vary. I told him not to use scare tactics to keep them from parting, and to allow those who desire to leave the ministry to depart freely with his good prayers and blessings, as Lot parted from Abraham without being cursed, criticized, or condemned. I continued that he must always bear in mind that the people in his ministry belong to God and are lent to him to love, build up, encourage, and unite with, and when people leave his ministry, they leave mainly for these two core reasons: purposed and nonpurposed motives.

If you pray for and bless those who leave without a purpose, they will freely return without a guilty conscience and without feeling ashamed. But, those Josephs (the son of Jacob) in ministry will depart with a purpose, and God may not reveal to the leader the reason for their untimely parting.

I expressed to this pastor that ministry is like an elevator ride that starts on the ground floor. There are those who will start with you but will get off on the fifth floor; but keep in mind there will be more who will get on the elevator from the fifth floor, just as there will be people who will continually get on/off on different floors. But you will have some who started with you from the ground floor and ride with you the whole time. This example is not about those who are/were faithful or unfaithful, but about purposed and nonpurposed motives.

I also told him that ministry is like a bus, with him being the primary bus driver (as assigned and directed by God). He must allow people to freely get on/get off the bus, as his sole purpose should be teaching, building, and edifying the current group of people riding the bus, while simultaneously staying focused on driving the bus.

And lastly, ministry is like school (God being the superintendent and his called leaders being the teachers/counselors). There will be those who will begin with you at the elementary level, then are purposed to continue elsewhere (in another district) as they transit to intermediate, high school, and the college level. And some will drop out of school altogether. Make yourself available for those who dropped out without a purpose – for some will return to school in hopes of earning their GED and your support will be vital for their success. The bottom line is, let people freely come and go as you continue to be who God fashioned you to become and you allow God to be who He is – the Author and Finisher of our faith.

God is still working on all of us as a depiction of His temple/His building as he continues to repair the breaches and broken places in our lives. Being a Christian is not about masking your true identity, but accepting who you are and where you are in life with transparency. Some of the challenges many have in Christianity is that we have not yet revealed our faces from behind the veil, displaying our weaknesses without pretending to be invincible and above reproach, taking pleasure in concealing our uniqueness. True salvation gives us freedom from masking our shame from past/present sins, as Adam did in covering himself with fig leaves, but God replaced the fig leaves and exchanged them for coats of animal skins that entirely covered both

Adam's and Eve's bodies. I would like to include this thought regarding Adam and Eve by noting that even in their wrongdoing they displayed togetherness and unity. A man/woman who is married is wedded to that person and not the church (the physical structure of the building/its people). God's idea of marriage is not that a man/woman should leave his/her spouse and cleave/cling to the place/house of worship, yet this is what many believe and behave accordingly. I have seen countless numbers of married couples allow their marriages to split based on the words of a spiritual leader, with one party agreeing while the other party is in disagreement with the leader.

A team wins together and loses together and marriage is about winning/losing together. It's about unifying and not dividing – for division is not marriage but divorce, which means to disassociate, disconnect, and detach, and God has not instituted this thing called "marriage" to end in tragedy based on another man's/woman's view. People divorce for many different reasons (and some reasons are permitted and legitimate).

Final Analysis: Real Talk

God permitted Moses to write a bill of divorcement for reasons such as adultery, infidelity, etc., but never allow your marriage to be severed because of the influence of another man/woman, whether that man/woman is of great reputation, or whether they are a spiritual leader or not.

When my wife and I were in the engagement stage of our relationship, our agreement of marriage and love for each other was not based upon the opinions of others but on genuine love, and it is that same genuine love that keeps us united during the tough times of disagreement and disappointment. Although Adam and Eve fell short of God's covenant, they were jointly unsuccessful and mutually covered by God's grace, and together aided in the population of the whole earth.

Abraham hearkened unto the voice of his wife Sarah who encouraged him to have sex with her handmaid and Ishmael was born. Ishmael, who was not the seed that God had promised from the loins of Abraham and Sarah, relentlessly quarreled with Isaac, who was the son of promise. It was the same Sarah who urged Abraham to release Hagar and Ishmael from their duties and responsibilities, isolating them from the rest of the family unit. Although Abraham initially disagreed, God sided with Sarah because of His ultimate purpose for Isaac. Mistakes are part of marriage, but love and unity can shelter and expunge many blunders. The same is true for those who are single.

Your love and unity with God can be a refuge and safe haven from the sinful nature of humanity, even those who represent one thing but live in total opposition to what they represent (masking their true nature). Living a life of Christianity can be tough at times, as was displayed in the life of Christ, but the key to avoiding bitterness in your relationship with God and ministry is allowing the Almighty be the focal point in your life and not just a place on Sunday morning or a prayer in times of trouble.

In this relationship we are obliged to learn of him, know him, and display his attributes, which are humanly unattainable, but possible through Christ. Becoming knowledgeable in Christ and learning His ways is not about faithfully attending church every day/every Sunday: it's not about having titles/and being called upon, and it's not being the pastor's favorite member. It's about spending time in His word, in prayer, and in His presence.

By doing this, we will have the wisdom and guidance to manage life and all we put our hands toward, as it will also aid us in enduring life's unfortunate troubles. This is not suggesting you disregard God's leaders, but this is a way to keep things in proper perspective: love and embrace your leaders, but serve, praise, and worship the Lord our God. This will help you more as servants in the body of Christ and lessen your chance of becoming a servant to man's agenda.

We are all members of one body and that body is no other than the body of Christ, who died for our sins but was raised again for our justification and validation. For those who have been hurt in or by ministry, or hurt by a trusted leader, whether it was physical abuse, sexual abuse, emotional or social abuse, it's time to let the healing began to illuminate your life and saturate you soul – first by asking God to forgive you for being bitter with Him, and secondly by asking Christ to restore the joy of your salvation. If all possible, this process of healing may also include reconciliation with and forgiveness towards the abuser. The heinous things that transpired during your time in ministry were indeed ugly and immoral, but now it's time to allow God to use those things to inspire and encourage others who crossed those same paths. However this time, in your new or restored journey with Christ, you must comprehend that the religious traditional way of thinking must be modified and altered.

God is not doing the same things in the identical manner as before; he is preparing you for a whole different expedition as fully directed by and through his Word – not regulated by customary apostolic protocols and conventions but through His pure and unadulterated Word. God did not purpose us to be ensnared in wrongdoing, but as with Adam and Eve; we were deceived when we took our eyes off God and replaced him with something or someone with similar likeness. And God doesn't command us to pretend that the hardships we faced in ministry never happened. It is His will for us to get up, learn from our mistakes, continue fighting the good fight of faith, and support others in similar situations.

When I was ensnared with deception in ministry; with the psychological and sexual abuse, the moment I regained clear consciousness and vision, I was somewhat bitter with man and ministry, and somewhat apprehensive of Christianity and religion. But the one thing I didn't do was turn my back against the one who is the giver of life and the one who is the eternal hope for humanity. Once the enemy (the spirit of wickedness) convinces you that God is at fault, and you lose all hope and confidence in God, where else can you turn to for security and help? Whom can you trust? Who is greater in stature than God? Where else can you go? Whom can you lean on when the solid rock has sunken in your life?

It is the job of the enemy to not only get us to lose hope in Christian leaders or religious leaders in general, but also for us to visualize God as hopeless. Once that occurs, you'll have a long road ahead to regain your trust in God. But it's not impossible. With man it's impossible, but with/through God all things are possible. Furthermore, by not being bitter with God (through my hardships), I was able to see clearly the mistakes I made, as well as the mistakes I allowed others to make for me in my life. I've been able to forgive, which is one of the greatest keys to recovery, and able to embrace the past and present with great expectancy of my future.

My relationship with Christ has grown in leaps and bounds for both me and my wife. We have continued to trust and believe in God, despite life's disappointments. Now we both truly know that it is through our weaknesses that Christ was most revealed – in those hard places of brokenness.

Many will read this and suppose I am angry and bitter with leadership in the body of Christ, but I myself am a leader and teacher of the gospel of Jesus Christ; an evangelist to lost and misguided souls. No, I am not livid, just more aware and enlightened in the realm of Christianity and will not accept anything less than the truth or that which is real. I understand that I'm not here on earth to please man, but I'm here to please God and to love, support, and work in unity with those who believe in and love the aspects of His truth.

I am reminded about the passage of scripture where Christ called Lazarus forth from the grave; but his face was yet draped with grave linen: he was FREE BUT YET BOUND; and although Christ have freed us from the penalty of sin (which is death); as with Lazarus, he also desire that we be free from burial wrappings or those things that burden us with pain (St. John 11:43-44).

True healing that comes from Christ through God is not about training our minds to ignore and mask the pain of tragedy through religion by just moving on; but not moving forward. True healing is about recognition, it's about acknowledgement, it's about being nursed back to health (physical & spiritual) so that the injury of misfortune no longer have power over us.

Do not live the rest of your life to the bondage of man, but in the freedom and sovereignty of Christ. Don't allow other people's ignorance to keep you from trusting, loving, and living for God once more. For God is too good to forget; and too real to ignore. Allow God to restore your true self and your spiritual health so that you can avoid or overcome the bitterness of Christianity that mankind has made it to appear; although Christianity in its purest devotion, is the best thing that ever happened to both me and you.

As the Apostle Jude concluded in his letter to the believers in Christ found in the book of Jude 1:24-25:

"Now to Him who is able to keep us from slipping and to present us unblemished and blameless in the midst of His presence and glory with triumphant joy, to the only prudent God, our Savior through Jesus Christ our Lord, be grandeur, dignity, dominion, and supremacy: both now in the present as well as the future for all periods of eternity. Amen."

www.ingramcontent.com/pod-product-compliance
Lightning Source LLC
LaVergne TN
LVHW051545070426
835507LV00021B/2407